TALKING BACK TO GOD

TALKING
BACK TO
GOD

SPEAKING YOUR HEART TO GOD
THROUGH THE PSALMS

LYNN ANDERSON

LEAFWOOD
PUBLISHERS
an imprint of Abilene Christian University Press

Talking Back To God
Speaking Your Heart to God through the Psalms

an imprint of Abilene Christian University Press

Copyright 2010 by Lynn Anderson

ISBN 978-0-89112-646-1
LCCN 2010012774

Printed in the United States of America

LIBRARY OF CONGRESS CATALOGING-IN-PUBLICATION DATA
Anderson, Lynn, 1936-
Talking back to God : speaking your heart to God through the Psalms / Lynn Anderson.
   p. cm.
ISBN 978-0-89112-646-1
1. Bible. O.T. Psalms--Devotional use. I. Title.
BS1430.55.A63 2010
242'.5--dc22
   2010012774

Cover design by Marc Whitaker
Interior text design by Sandy Armstrong, Strong Design

Leafwood Publishers is an imprint of Abilene Christian University Press
ACU Box 29138
Abilene, Texas 79699

1-877-816-4455
www.leafwoodpublishers.com

To John and Evelyn Willis
My mentors and heroes of the faith
who first introduced me to praying the Psalms

CONTENTS

INTRODUCTION

When Michelangelo finished his colossal sculpture of King David, legend has it that he made a last tap with the chisel, leaned in and blew away the dust then stepped back and said, "Speak to me."

I doubt that many authors ever come to Michelangelo's strong sense of closure. Rather, in the end, they send off to press a book that they feel is still "a work in progress." This book represents my current stage of the journey.

I'll never forget the first time I visited the Academy of the Arts in Florence, Italy and looked down the long hallway. There stood Michelangelo's King David, and it took my breath away. Of course, the marble could not truly speak actual words to Michelangelo, but that incredible sculpture "spoke" powerfully to me that day.

Even more powerful than this sculpture is another ancient masterpiece—yet it is also a work in progress. For three thousand years the voices of David and other psalmists have been speaking. And ever since those words were first preserved in songs and writings, people have been talking back to God using the Psalms.

The Psalms are a place where contemporaries meet the ancients as we all try to account for the chaos, suffering, celebration, and lament we feel in our lives. The 150 psalms that make up the book of Psalms are not only God's word to us, but also humanity's words spoken back to God. When we read, sing, memorize, and pray the Psalms, we are doing so with faithful people seeking God, past and present.

Have you ever felt like talking back to God? If so, you're in good company with people through the ages who have been using the Psalms or creating their own psalms as a way to talk back to God. This book is a humble guide for talking back to God using the Psalms.

What you will find here are my insights—gained over several decades—about pursuing God using the Psalms. These ancient Psalms have shaped my life and my discipleship more than any other collection of writings in or outside the Bible. Not only that, but I also use the Psalms to mentor others. And now, after all these years, the Psalms are mentoring me through one of the roughest patches of my life.

Why have the Psalms shaped me so much? Why have they been so important to people of faith through the ages? Because they speak to the hunger we have for God and put us in touch with our desire to pursue and talk back to him. As Augustine said, addressing God, "Our hearts are restless till they find rest in you." The Lord put this gnawing hunger in us so we would search for him.

Living in the Psalms has been a great adventure into worlds unimagined. The Psalms are pathways into the heart of God prepared by people—we call them "psalmists"—who hunger and thirst for the living God. They give us words to pray when we can't find any.

Moving through the Psalms is like a pilgrimage into the heart of God. Pilgrimages move people physically closer to a holy place. The whole journey—not just the arrival—is a pursuit of God. The Psalms pilgrimage moves us through emotional and spiritual deserts, mountains, waters, and valleys. One terrain the Psalms seem particularly familiar with is the desert—those dry times when all seems hopeless and death certain. When we pursue God in the Psalms, we find pools of refreshing water on the journey, even in the desert.

One psalm in particular provides a guiding metaphor for our pilgrimage. Psalm 84:6 shows pilgrims traveling through the dry Valley of Baca to Jerusalem. One definition of the Hebrew word "Baca" is bitterness. God-hungry people all stream into the city from different directions, and some must pass through the valley of bitterness.

But as they approach the city where they intend to worship the Lord in the Temple, they find what the psalmist calls "pools of autumn rain." Those who successfully pass through, year after year, often find these pools of autumn rain where once was only a desert. They begin to see the way God has provided for them and even shown his glory to them in the wilderness journey before arriving in Jerusalem. They conclude that one day in the presence of God is better than a thousand elsewhere.

These pools in the Valley of Baca are a metaphor of the Psalms. The pools remind us of God's presence along the journey. The Psalms are like these pools of autumn rain. As autumn rains refresh the desperate pilgrim in the Valley of Baca, so also the Psalms lead us on a hopeful pilgrimage toward the heart of God.

For decades I have prayed and sung the Psalms. Years ago, some speaking assignments nudged me into a yearlong and life-changing adventure with the Psalms. I lived for one year in the Psalms, praying five psalms every day. I did not just read through them; I wallowed down into them, and most days, stayed there till God showed up—or rather, I showed up to pay attention to God! During this period, I set my heart to memorize a psalm each month.

Since that year of living in the Psalms, I still return there day after day and commit psalms to memory and use them to minister to others. That year of praying the Psalms was a real, red-blooded spiritual adventure. In the years since, most of the time I have prayed one psalm a day and memorized one psalm a month (not every day, not every month, but most of the time). My journey and this book flow out of that watershed year in pursuit of God through the Psalms. And my prayer is that it will help you pursue God as well.

If you genuinely want a fresh approach to pursuing God, the most traveled and proven prayer path is the Psalms. If you start up this road, however, be prepared to go beyond merely *reading* the Psalms. Be prepared to wallow in them and pay attention to what God is doing in your life and in the world.

In the following chapters, you will find a pathway into the Psalms, a pilgrimage into reading, praying, singing, memorizing, and ministering through which you can encounter the same God the psalmists encountered. Each chapter includes exercises of Reflection and Action that gently raise the bar of challenge and expectation—leading those who feel so called to become trainers of others in the Psalms journey.

The Psalms supply pools of autumn rain that give us "strength upon strength" till we pilgrims all come face to face with God. As the psalmist says in Psalm 84:5-7,

Blessed are those whose strength is in you,
who have set their hearts on pilgrimage.
As they pass through the Valley of Baca,
they make it a place of springs;
the autumn rains also cover it with pools.
They go from strength to strength,
till each appears before God in Zion.

This portion of Psalm 84 is my prayer for you as you strike out on your journey in the Psalms and into the heart of God. As the book of Psalms becomes our songbook and prayer book, these psalms add freshness, variety, and depth to our souls as our hearts cry out for the living God.

From what we can gather about the mysterious Almighty, he really is listening to our prayers. In our psalms to him, he even finds pleasure and does not remain unmoved. Getting the answers we want in prayer is missing the point. Instead, God allows us to talk back to him and encounter him in a loving relationship. That paradox of a holy God engaging our finite human lives is worth more than a thousand answers to a thousand prayers.

Are you ready to talk back to God?

PART I

HUNGER

Chapter 1

HUNGERING FOR GOD

"I only pray when I am in trouble.
But I am in trouble all the time, and so I pray all the time." [1]
—Isaac Bashevis Singer

A dozen Christian leaders circled around a table one morning as we discussed our hunger for God.

During the conversation that day, we spoke of "encounter with God" as the ultimate goal of humanity, a deep and growing relationship with God that changes us. Yet, talking about encounter with God brought a mood that was not triumphant and pious but pensive and thick.

Why? What was preventing those in the group that day from filling their hunger for God?

"I hate to admit it," James confessed, "but sometimes my schedule gets so hectic I don't even pray much for days, so I don't encounter God in any personal or meaningful way." Several nodded their heads from more than simple courtesy—it seemed they identified with James. But each had a different perspective.

"My problem is a bit different," Carole said. "I usually reach out for God fairly regularly. But my devotional life often feels stale and I sink into this rut, praying the same old things every day. Sometimes I feel as if God is hiding from me," she said.

Clarke agreed. "I hear that. Rote, stale, and repetitive. Plus, my prayers become narrower and narrower. Here lately I pray mostly about me: my needs, my family, and my job. Me! So I feel at times I pay far more attention to myself than to God!"

James, Carole, and Clarke—these are not their real names, but this is a common conversation that took place in my mentoring groups. Each of us seems to hunger for God, but our pace, our stale prayers, or our own selfishness inhibits us from encountering him. And here's the kicker. These friends around the table that day—each feeling hectic, stale, selfish feelings of distance from God—are widely respected Christian leaders! And even though they have deep faith, they still struggle and find themselves stuck and reaching out for God from the hungering depths of their souls.

What about you? You may be a Christian leader, a person of deep conviction, yet your prayers are stale because of your hectic pace. Or perhaps you have distanced yourself from God because of a traumatic event that left you cold. You have no words to pray. Everything you've tried still comes up short.

But let's not fool ourselves. The problem is not solely the lack of good prayer habits or practices. The problem often begins with ignoring the gnawing emptiness that is a hunger for God. Perhaps because of the pressures of life, we reach for quick fillers for the void that only God can satisfy. So our biggest challenge may be learning how to pay attention to our hunger pains for the living God.

The Psalms help us pay attention. One hundred and fifty psalms were collected as a prayer book for the Hebrew people and handed down for three thousand years. These Psalms have been prayed, sung, copied, memorized, paraphrased, shouted, and whispered for thirty centuries as humanity attempts to make sense of the chaos of life and pay attention to what God is doing in the world.

The Psalms help us make sense of our experiences, yet the Psalms wrap no gifts with a neat little bow, give no easy answers. They do, however, speak to the rawness of life where these dilemmas are found. And they show us that in these places we can discover God's presence.

The reason I'm so excited about you reading this book is because the main idea parallels the goal of our lives: encountering God and his loving, transforming presence.

In pursuing God, we first come to terms with our human condition. That is, when we discover our hunger for God, we learn how to fill ourselves with God, not everything else. Our circumstances can drive a wedge between God and us—or they can draw us closer. That's one reason why the Psalms are so important in the pursuit of God: they address the human condition so well and get us ready to encounter God in any life situation.

Walter Brueggemann says the Psalms speak to three major conditions of humanity, this "common lot" we share with each other. He says the life of faith consists of moving with God in the following life situations:

1. Times when we are securely oriented.
2. Times when we are painfully disoriented.
3. Times when we are surprisingly reoriented.

The Psalms are the voice of ancient faith talking back to God. How can we identify with those words when they are so distant and ancient? Is it possible to join these ancient voices and make them our own? We can identify with these ancient voices because they reflect the ups and downs of life as we experience it. Sometimes we feel secure. So when we read Psalm 8, we hear a securely oriented voice: "Oh Lord, how majestic is your name in all the earth!" When we're painfully disoriented, we can identify with the disoriented voice of Psalm 88: "Darkness is my closest friend." And when we find ourselves surprisingly reoriented, feeling God's fresh presence, we can read Psalm 118: "Give thanks to the LORD, for he is good; his love endures forever."

When we fall in line with society's lock-step rhythms, the Psalms can break us out of this awful spell. As Walter Brueggemann says in his book, *Praying the Psalms,*

In most arenas where we live, we are expected and required to speak the language of safe orientation and equilibrium, either to find it so or to pretend we find it so. For the normal, conventional functioning of public life, the raw edges of disorientation and reorientation must be denied or suppressed for purposes of public equilibrium. As a result, our speech is dulled and mundane. Our passion has been stilled and is without imagination. And mostly the Holy One is not addressed—not because we dare not, but because God is far away and hardly seems important. This means the agenda and intention of the Psalms is considerably at odds with the normal speech of most people, the normal speech of a stable, functioning, self-deceptive culture in which everything must be kept running young and smooth. [2]

So when we think we are securely oriented, that can be a façade, a reliance on the economy, government, our education, our families, even our churches. In that kind of security we easily get sidetracked and ignore God. This leads to praying mostly about surface issues. We pray a laundry list of self-centered petitions rather than paying attention to God. This leaves us panting for air and spinning our wheels. We're still hungry for God.

Most of the Psalms speak to us out of the situation of disorientation. For those of us inexperienced in or opposed to questioning God, the Psalms become a great guide to talking back to God. Even on our worst of days. Indeed, most of all on those days.

Once we learn to pay attention to our hunger for God, we can then acknowledge our pangs and cry out to the One who can fill us. There is a big difference between crying out for all the answers you want in prayer and crying out for the loving presence of the living God. The former is crying out to be filled with all that we think we need: money, relationships, prestige, and power. The latter is crying out to God to fill us with himself.

Are these challenges—these roadblocks to pursuing God—inevitable in our life of prayer? Maybe not. Part of the problem could be flawed approaches to God and distorted expectations from prayer. We may be attempting quick fixes that cannot keep us out of the ditches. Do we always expect some kind of sensational experiences with God, or do we quietly pay attention to his presence?

The Psalms lead us to talk and to listen, to look and hear and feel God's presence, his voice. The Psalms magnify the reality of God's presence by exploring openly who God really is and what he is doing in the world. The paradox of poetry in the Psalms is a cadence we need in our lives.

Evil is all around us.

God is here.

Life is falling apart.

God is here.

In the fast pace of life, we tend to ignore God as well as the significance of this cadence of the Psalms that reminds us that the happiness we seek in so many ways is found only in God and God alone.

Pursuing God is infinitely better than pursuing happiness! If only we could get to a place where we abandon the pursuit of our own happiness and strike out on the adventure of pursuing God. If we pursue God as the adventure of our lives, we would experience a tectonic shift in our world—a deeper joy than the pursuit of happiness. This pursuit is expressed in the Psalms—a desire for more than the world can deliver.

Do you want to encounter God? Has your hunger for God been satisfied with things other than God? For centuries, spiritual leaders have paid attention to God and entered into the faith adventure using the Psalms. The Psalms show us how spiritual leaders dealt with pain and suffering, joy and celebration, ridicule and death-threats, doubt and darkness. We have much to learn from the Psalms and those spiritual leaders who put their relationship with God into poetic words for worshipers to experience with them. Spiritual leaders are the kind of people whom God-hungry people want to be like. A physically fit and healthy person models a lifestyle others want to live. Similarly, people want to be like spiritual leaders who regularly encounter God. So this journey into the Psalms also takes us to a place where we learn how to mentor others as well.

We want to see others model what it means to walk in the valley of the shadow of death and yet fear no evil. We benefit by watching people celebrate the creation story and all God has done for us. We listen to Psalms of passion for God and soak in the passion of others. The Psalms can become a primary tool for us to pay attention to God and pursue him.

In the next few chapters, the journey takes us beyond stale prayer gimmicks to a deeper understanding of what it means to be spiritually formed and transformed. The Psalms open a pathway to this life change.

Reflection

1. What do you think about the following quote by Isaac Bashevis Singer? "I only pray when I am in trouble. But I am in trouble all the time, and so I pray all the time"?

2. Do you feel that you are frequently in times of trouble?

3. What kinds of prayer help you encounter God in these times?

Action

1. Make a list of the things you have tried in order to come closer to God.

2. Which ones were most helpful in encountering God?

3. Why do you think some "worked" better than others?

Chapter 2

PAYING ATTENTION

*To reject the spiritual disciplines wholesale is to insist that
growth in the spirit is something that just happens all by itself.
But when a believer does reject them, he or she must then
assume the responsibility of putting other effective spiritual
disciplines in their place.*[1]

—Dallas Willard

Our restless hearts will not find rest in prayer gimmicks or the latest fad. And the habits of prayer must replace the habit of not praying. Talking back to God using the Psalms helps us move from prayer gimmicks to productive habits.

Some people experiment with one gimmick after another to make prayer work. For example, New Year's resolutions don't typically help because we rarely keep them. Even if we do stick with them, our hearts often go numb by February. Or maybe you have set your watch to beep and remind you when it is your "quiet time." Or you have tried standing, jogging, or peddling an exercise bike to stay alert during prayer. Or maybe you pray during drive time, turning those annoying red traffic lights into "calls to prayer." Or maybe you've filled each calendar day with a person to pray for that day. You could make your own list of prayer methods, but you have likely discovered that those methods that seem helpful in the short run seldom sustain a lasting and vibrant sense of God's presence in your life.

Gimmicks won't get it. Believe me. I know. I've tried them. I understand your struggle with prayer, with hunger for God on a long journey. I still struggle and still find many of these roadblocks along the way.

I've tried dogged disciplines and found they don't last if we still "sit outside" the prayers we pray. What does that mean? It means we can pray regularly, but if the goal is not intentionally encountering God, we are only spinning our wheels and "sitting outside" the prayers we pray. We haven't yet entered into the presence of God. So we must somehow find our way into the spirit of our devotional disciplines where communion with God becomes increasingly real.

Along the journey, the roadblocks to prayer sometimes deflect us into the ditches. Some have pitched out routine altogether because they feel this leads them only to fall into a rut. Others have too much routine because they fear letting go of their walking stick and skipping along the path of prayer. Is there some kind of centering balance to be found in our prayer lives?

To keep our physical balance, we need an internal support system. When something goes wrong with our inner ear or a medication affects our body functioning, we can lose our sense of balance. We teeter to one side, even fall. Likewise, in order to keep our spiritual balance along the journey, to stay between the ditches, we need balanced prayer practices. On the one hand, it would be disastrous to expect to keep one's spiritual life fresh and one's sense of God's presence alive without any form of regular, meaningful prayer. On the other hand, it is of little value merely to latch onto a borrowed prayer gimmick or routine.

I remember a time in our parenting saga when our four children were elementary to high school ages. Some of you can imagine the scene. Some of you don't want to! Raising four children, we were long past man-to-man defense and had gone to zone coverage. Life was definitely an adventure without even trying. But we wanted the kind of adventure God wanted, not the kind born of chaos and come what may.

So Carolyn and I determined we would set a regular time for "family devotions." When that time rolled around, we would turn off the television and gather for the family devotional time. Never mind if it was in the middle of the kids' favorite television program, we'd turn it off and say, "Okay, it's devo time now." Can you imagine what a warm receptive frame of mind this created for our kids? They would moan and turn the television off, but they would scarcely be in a good frame of mind for devotionals. Why? We didn't set the mood for a devotion to God because we often left them in the middle of the show's cliffhanger.

So at times, our desire for strong spiritual practices in our home became a barrier on our spiritual journey. Yet I would not change a thing—well, maybe I'd let the kids see how their show ends! The reason I would change little is because we do need spiritual practices. I might change the way we did the routine but not the practice of Bible reading and prayer. The routines and practices lead us to something much bigger, an adventure better than any television show, to a God who loves us beyond our wildest imagination and in our worst moments.

Our children are grown now, and we have grandchildren who need these routines too. We see our children repeating some of these routines in their own homes. My daughter Debbie shared with me that she really did hear and appreciate our Bible reading every morning when we sat down to breakfast. She said she may have rolled her eyes or tried to act as if she wasn't interested, but she was. Indeed, the word rests on our hearts, as the rabbis say, until our hearts are broken enough for the word to enter.

Not just families but whole churches can fail at this balance. They often react to traditional practices within their denomination and swing far the other way, doing even more damage to the flock. In his book, *Spirit of the Disciplines*, Dallas Willard says that many have reacted so strongly to legalism and asceticism that they have a cheap view of the abundant life. He sees whole churches expecting less and less discipleship. They expect the abundant life without the very spiritual disciplines that would bring them life. It's like expecting to have big muscles without vigorous workouts at the gym.

We need some kind of balance between a rigid asceticism—spirituality of extreme self-denial—and cheap spirituality. Rigid asceticism leads to one kind of worship God hates: lip service. And cheap spirituality leads to another kind of religious activity God hates: amassing abundance while others suffer.

An important way to get past gimmicks, guilt, and cheap methods is to come to God as we are. Rich or poor, hungry or well fed, happy or sad, healthy or sick, we come to God. If we approach him with a cover-up, we will not be able to encounter God in a way that really changes our lives. What if young shepherd David had worn King Saul's armor to face Goliath? Saul's kind of armor was the conventional uniform for soldiers in battle. But it did not fit David.

We sometimes lose the God-encountering prayer battle because we are attempting to fight our giants with someone else's ill-fitting armor. Someone else's disciplines may not fit you or me. We may doggedly clone another person's devotional mechanics and still not connect with God.

Remember the mentoring circle I told you about earlier in the book? At our discussion table that day with a group of Christian leaders, Clarke piped up again, "Yeah, I've been fooled by a bunch of those gimmicks. But to be honest, some techniques have really helped. For example, being part of a small accountability group helps me keep my journey with God on track."

The circle of friends agreed that they found it nearly impossible even to stay spiritually alive—much less to flourish—without the support and accountability of a small group.

But Clarke threw in a caution. "Yes, my group does keep me consistent, but it doesn't necessarily keep me sensitive to God's presence, and keep my prayers fresh."

"Every time I walk into a Christian bookstore," Jim added, "I see a new batch of stuff on drawing close to God. I've found some of these resources helpful to a point. For example, you've likely used the A.C.T.S. prayer formula: Adoration. Confession. Thanksgiving. Supplication."

Jim went on to explain that this prayer formula helped him remember to pray for someone beside himself but didn't keep his prayers from being narrow and repetitious. The group kicked around several helpful devotional methods that day, agreeing that most of them might be of some value—at certain places along the journey. But they also agreed that, at best, humanly generated prayer forms are always limited and eventually grow stale.

We're not all wired up alike, so mimicking another person's devotional disciplines is risky. A prayer formula that helped me may not help you at all. Even authors of sure-fire devotional manuals move past what they recommend. By the time we read their book, they discover the next level of their own spiritual development. Prayer techniques which at first look like the highways to holiness often turn out to be merely blind alleys. In other words, a formula prayed regularly gives us an impression of spirituality but can shut off our sense for what is happening in the world.

"So is it hopeless then?" Joe asked the group? He was one of the quieter members of the group. "Can nothing be done to keep our prayer lives fresh and vibrant? And to help us regularly encounter the Almighty?"

Daunting question—but the punch line is that we've been carrying around the answer in our hands, in the pages of Scripture, and in our hearts all along. God has given us something so obvious that it's as clear and big and refreshing as the Montana sky.

Paying attention to our hunger for God and launching into the adventure is the first big step toward pursuing God. When we recognize this hunger is a desire God has put in our hearts for himself, we begin to open ourselves to ways of encountering him that have endured since the first days of creation. We move beyond gimmicks and gadgets of prayer and into the ambiguity, mystery, and beauty of a relationship that is not contained in techniques but unleashed in our lives as a quest for God himself.

The next stage along this adventure of pursuing God is to enter the Psalms yourself or as a family, group, or church. Seriously consider entering the Psalms with no agenda but to seek God there.

The Bible is not God but helps us seek him. So here's one way to think of entering a portion of Scripture such as the Psalms. In most Bibles, the Psalms are found near the center when you open the book by dividing the pages evenly on left and right. Imagine when you open the Psalms that you are centering and entering a portal into the immense life and heart of God.

At the same time, when you open Scripture, visualize your own heart and life opening. That's how I moved beyond gimmicks of prayer: I started entering the Psalms with an open heart to find God and talk back to him. I began with the Psalms as they are, then I brought my own experience to them, and finally started praying them, singing them, memorizing them, and ministering with them.

The mentoring circle I've been telling you about confessed their anemic prayer lives and barriers on the path to encountering God. Toward evening in that mentoring meeting, the group challenged each other to pray five psalms a day for one month. Having prayed through the 150 psalms in one month, we would then pray one psalm a day for the rest of the year. That one-psalm-a-day year proved to be incredibly important for the group—and for me.

What about you? Maybe your prayers and pursuit of God is full of life and joy and even lament. Perhaps you already know how anemic your prayer life is and you are ready to confess you feel far from God. Would you take the challenge and make this same commitment as the group did that day? Yes, a commitment like this calls for investment of time and energy, but pursuing God in this way is well worth the effort. Many of us spend more time with various media than with Scripture, and we need ways to re-center our lives on God. This practice will help you do that.

One problem we face when we enter the Bible—or more specifically, the Psalms—is that we are uncertain where to start and where to finish. One simple way to enter the Psalms is to read five psalms a day. This takes us through the Book of Psalms once a month. But this can be an intimidating way to begin. So why not begin by reading just one psalm today? Then read another psalm tomorrow and one each day.

Do not concern yourself about missing days or trying to catch up. Concentrate less on how much you read and more on how deep into a psalm you penetrate, how close to the heart of God. There's no reading schedule to catch up on—only catch up to God in today's psalm.

The Psalms draw us into holy encounter with God. Wow! I do not know anyone who has followed this path and ended up disillusioned or even disappointed. God's solution to your prayer problems may actually be this obvious, this ancient, this profoundly simple.

Would you simply enter the Psalms today? Open your Bible and open your heart and read a psalm today. Commit each day to opening your Bible and your heart. Some days these psalms will only just rest *on* your heart. But when your heart breaks open, the word enters.

If you are still wondering how to begin, here's a psalm that embodies the journey of faith we've been discussing. Psalm 90 is attributed to Moses. Many people think David wrote all of the Psalms. He did write roughly half of them, but many other psalmists, including the Sons of Korah, Ethan the Ezrahite, Moses, and Asaph wrote psalms as well. They wrote psalms of praise, lament, ascent to the Temple, vengeance, and many more.

Psalm 90 begins the fourth of five sections that divide the Book of Psalms. This psalm can be our prayer for the journey together into the heart of God using the Psalms.

A prayer of Moses the man of God.

Lord, you have been our dwelling place
    throughout all generations.
Before the mountains were born
    or you brought forth the earth and the world,
    from everlasting to everlasting you are God.
You turn men back to dust,
    saying, "Return to dust, O sons of men."
For a thousand years in your sight
    are like a day that has just gone by,
    or like a watch in the night.
You sweep men away in the sleep of death;
    they are like the new grass of the morning—
though in the morning it springs up new,
    by evening it is dry and withered.
We are consumed by your anger
    and terrified by your indignation.
You have set our iniquities before you,
    our secret sins in the light of your presence.

All our days pass away under your wrath;
    we finish our years with a moan.
The length of our days is seventy years—
    or eighty, if we have the strength;
    yet their span is but trouble and sorrow,
    for they quickly pass, and we fly away.
Who knows the power of your anger?
    For your wrath is as great as the fear that is due you.
Teach us to number our days aright,
    that we may gain a heart of wisdom.
Relent, O LORD! How long will it be?
    Have compassion on your servants.
Satisfy us in the morning with your unfailing love,
    that we may sing for joy and be glad all our days.
Make us glad for as many days as you have afflicted us,
    for as many years as we have seen trouble.
May your deeds be shown to your servants,
    your splendor to their children.
May the favor of the Lord our God rest upon us;
    establish the work of our hands for us—
    yes, establish the work of our hands.

After all these centuries, we can still meaningfully pray this psalm of Moses. That's how durable the Psalms are for the pursuit of God and in understanding our world. In the next chapter, we'll explore more ancient words that have incredibly contemporary application. Across many cultures and across time, people have talked back to God using these words as the forms of speech that express their deepest longings, their highest celebrations, and their most earnest prayers.

As we continue, may the favor of the Lord our God be upon us and establish the work of our hands.

Reflection

1. What do you think about this statement by Dallas Willard? "To reject the spiritual disciplines wholesale is to insist that growth in the spirit is something that just happens all by itself."

2. What are ways you have rejected spiritual disciplines?

3. What spiritual disciplines have you accepted and practiced?

Action

1. Choose one psalm to read today.

2. Read the psalm through one time.

3. Take a few minutes to sit quietly and let the psalm soak in.

4. Enjoy one psalm and try not to feel pressure to cover a lot of ground in the number of psalms you read. Go deeper rather than farther.

Chapter 3

LEARNING TO TALK

We search the world for good, we cull
The bright, the pure, the beautiful.
And weary seekers of the best,
We come home laden from our quest,
And find that all the sages said,
Was in the book our father's read. [1]
—Thomas Wolfe

The first time I was called to minister to a dying believer was in the tiny town of Tupelo, Arkansas in the fall of 1957. I was twenty-one years old, and as green as the woods surrounding that little village. Sensing my plight, the suffering sister sized me up and graciously intervened.

"Son, you don't know what to say, do you?" she said.

I felt speechless like a bashful child and this kind woman was lifting my chin up to look her directly in the eyes.

"No, Ma'am," I mumbled, "I don't."

"Then let's just read the Bible," she said.

She gently coached me to open the Scriptures and begin with the basics.

"Maybe you could begin with the twenty-third psalm," she said.

I read Psalm 23 and a peace settled over the room as she listened and variously nodded and smiled with a distant look in her eyes.

"The Lord is my shepherd, I shall not want," I read, and each line resonated with me, partly because I could see how it resonated with this dying sister in Christ.

I have read Psalm 23 hundreds of times since that day in Tupelo. I have read Psalm 23 at funerals and at happy occasions, in times of suffering and times of celebration. But never have I read Psalm 23 with more fervor than that autumn day in 1957. Psalm 23 became a pool of autumn rain for a dying woman walking through a dry and weary land. And I was there to witness the word penetrate her heart . . . even as it penetrated mine, too.

Even now, every time I read Psalm 23—or any psalm for that matter—I feel a fresh sense of wonder. One of the greatest lessons of ministry I learned, I didn't learn in a classroom or seminary. I didn't learn this lesson with bookshelves surrounding me in a library—yes, I did have great professors and a few great libraries in which to learn. But the lesson I learned on that day was one that would give me a ministry resource that has lasted five decades. Come to find out, this tool is an ancient one that God's people were using centuries before Christ.

The great lesson that began for me in 1957 with the faith of a sister in Christ who mentored me is still as true today as it has been for three millennia: *The Psalms teach us how to talk. By listening to these faithful voices, we learn to talk back to God.*

From that day in 1957, I set about to learn how to talk back to God. First, I learned to read the Psalms to others. I read to my family, to the churches I served, to people in the hospital, and at funerals. The Psalms became a go-to resource for ministry. But something was missing. I had not fully connected the Psalms to my own life.

Before long, I began to connect the words to songs that we often sing in our worship gatherings. It's amazing how many of the songs we sing, even today, come out of the Psalms. Not only did the ancient psalmists write poetry set to music. but Jews and Christians through the ages have continued this rich tradition. I began to notice songs such as Martin Luther's "A Mighty Fortress," a paraphrase of Psalm 46. Martin Luther, John Calvin, Isaac Watts, and many others wrote whole Psalters—these include psalms and instructions for worship liturgy— for their particular church traditions.

A turning point in discovering the power and benefits of the Psalms came when I learned that Psalms are also prayers. Not only can we pray these poetic prayers in the written form of the original, but we can also pray them through our own experiences, worded specifically for our situations but rooted in the ancient psalm.

Eventually I discovered that memorizing the Psalms is also a powerful tool for ministry. A man named Marlin Hoffman inspired me to memorize big chunks of Scripture. Marvin was a walking memory bank of the Bible, a living breathing Word of God. Some friends and I set out to memorize portions of Scripture, and psalms were some of my favorite to learn.

Memorizing the Psalms became a key part of the mentoring groups that I have lead for many years, and every time I entered a group and challenged them to enter the Psalms, I would discover them anew myself. When we read, sing, pray, even memorize the Psalms, incredible things happen in our lives. When we memorize psalms, even saturate our subconscious mind with psalms, fragments pop to mind at important ministry moments with surprising frequency.

Ancient words such as the Psalms are not just best because they are oldest. The Psalms also serve a vital function in our lives. The Psalms are a prayer book for the church, a hymnbook for the ages, a manual of sorts for talking back to God. But the Psalms are also one of the most tried and true ways to listen to other voices praying.

Toddlers first listen intently to voices all around them until they are able to utter words themselves. Imagine the wonder of learning to talk! Praying ancient words is like this miraculous growth process. By listening to psalmists pray, we learn to pray. So when we feel our hunger pains for God, the next action is to pay attention—to listen— and through hearing we learn to talk. Psalms help us learn to talk to God.

This is especially true of disciplines for the God-hungry. If we pay attention to these psalms that have outlived many superficial and trendy prayer paths across the centuries, we begin to see why they have been preserved. They have stood the test of time because they have been found helpful to believers in many times and cultures. They are helpful in the most important dynamic of our lives: our communication with God.

Lyrics from Michael W. Smith's song come to mind here:

Ancient words, ever true,

changing me, changing you.

Here we are, with humble hearts.

Oh, let the ancient words impart.[2]

Ancient words are often the very best and helpful for teaching us how to talk back to God—we not only learn from these historic voices, but we're also changed by these words.

Yet we often fail to listen to these important voices because hearing them requires patience. And we won't hear them if our ears are tuned only to life's shortcuts. Perhaps that's how we've missed something so huge. The time has come to pay attention to one thing virtually all the real giants of the faith—including Jesus—have in common: they all communed with God through the Psalms! Practicing the reading, singing, praying, and memorizing of the Psalms is the most ancient of the ancient practices.

The very structure of the Bible points to the importance of the Psalms. In the heart of the Bible is a collection of 150 Psalms that didn't get there by accident. Fragments of Psalms are also quoted in many books of the Bible. Is it any wonder that those slimmed-down pocket Bibles contain the New Testament—plus the Psalms? The fact that psalms flowed freely from the lips and pens of writers throughout the Scriptures shows how important this ancient form was to people across many centuries.

Is it truly possible to learn to speak by listening to voices of ancient people? Dietrich Bonhoeffer, in *Life Together*, says that when we come to the Psalms and pray them for ourselves, we might stumble over the experiences expressed there that we feel are not our own. But that's where our pursuit of God moves to a deeper level, beyond petitions for ourselves and into the life of the ancient faith.

When we come to psalms that express intense emotions, we are stumbling upon words that express humanity's deep longing for God. And when we read or pray these psalms ourselves, we often discover that we have those longings as well; we find that deep place inside of us that we didn't know was there or didn't want to face.

The authors of these timeless poems and songs did not hastily scribble them down on napkins during some rare moments of euphoric epiphany. Rather, God-thoughts filled the hearts of people and overflowed in psalms that were written over a long period of time. These psalms became the cry of their hearts until their praise, beseeching, and complaints were eventually distilled into intricately woven Hebrew poetic form. No more thoughtful reflections on God can be found—no more anguished or jubilant—than in the Psalms. For thirty centuries they have run deepest, hit truest, lasted longest, and risen as a central column of prayer, praise, and lament among the most passionate people of God.

In each of the psalms, human voices talk back to God. Psalms are primarily the voices of people expressing their faith. But the Psalms are also God's word to us—inspired and preserved by God as an incredible, continuing gift to his people for worship.

Chances are, you've read, sung, and memorized psalms before now. Perhaps you already know how powerful these ancient words can be in our lives today. Maybe you have never really sunk your teeth into a single psalm. In any case, let me point out that in learning to talk back to God, we exercise our faith, we grow spiritually.

When we learn to talk back to God, we also discover there is so much more to encountering God than petitioning him for what we want. Our voice changes. We move past prayer techniques, beyond religious formation to transformation into the image of God, the very likeness of Jesus Christ. God's desire is to transform us into his likeness, his image. So learning to talk back to God moves us toward the desire of God's heart.

How do we learn how to talk back to God? In the first two chapters, we saw the importance of recognizing our hunger for God and paying attention to God and how he can fill this hunger. In chapter two, I challenged you to read a psalm or segment of a psalm daily. The idea is for these readings to move toward deeper times of prayer, song, and memorization, then finally toward using psalms in ministry to others. In this way, we gradually increase the expectations we have of ourselves.

Another progression in reading one psalm a day is simple yet powerful: now move to reading the chosen psalm three times daily.

The first reading is to get the feel for what the psalm is about. Consider reading the psalm aloud. You might need to prepare a place where you feel at ease doing this if you are in earshot of others and you are supposed to be having a "quiet time." Reading the psalm aloud while you are alone does something similar to hearing the words read in a group. Our ears often process what our eyes may not. We look, listen, and learn to speak ourselves.

The second time through is to pray the psalm for yourself. You may have never directly prayed a psalm or done any activities outside of reading. So here is where it may become challenging. Push through the awkwardness of how it feels, because the rewards to your life and pursuit of God will be great if you use the Psalms for springboards into deeper prayer and relationship.

The third reading is for others. The prayer changes from first person to third person. Rather than praying "I," the prayer turns to praying for "he" or "she" or "they"—these are prayers for others in your life. This is when your awareness of God grows deeper and your awareness of others broader. Read the psalm slowly, aloud, reflectively, allowing it to be a springboard for the remaining prayers of the day.

Because our minds are conditioned to do things productively, we might bristle against repeating a reading three times. But this kind of repetition has been practiced in prayer and meditation throughout the ages. Below are three well-known examples of ways of prayer that can deepen our experiences in the Psalms or any readings from Scripture.

Lectio Divina. The ancient classical way of praying the actual words of Scripture is called Lectio Divina, Latin for "holy reading." The practice is to listen carefully to the words of Scripture. What I have just described to you above—the three readings of a psalm—is a form of Lectio Divina. The Psalms are some of the most used texts for Lectio Divina, but any Scripture text can be used for this form of prayer. The hallmarks of the practice are repetition of the text, meditation on its words, and praying with the goal of being shaped into the image of Jesus Christ. This kind of prayer comes more from the heart than from the brain. Pursuing the heart of God through Lectio Divina develops patience in an impatient world, slowly, reflectively waiting for the mood of the phrase from the text to fill our consciousness.

Breathing prayer. This form of prayer is simple but powerful. Practicing breathing prayer brings two phrases into focus by repeating one with each breath taken in, the other with each exhaled breath. One prayer often prayed this way goes like this when breathing in: "Lord Jesus, Son of God." When breathing out the prayer goes like this: "Have mercy on me a sinner." This simple form of prayer, repeated during a period of meditation, often becomes very powerful, centering, and energizing.

Silent and contemplative prayer. This form of prayer helps us listen to God. When we're hearing many voices all around us competing for our attention, silent and contemplative prayer moves us into a season of listening to God. Rather than filling our minds with concepts and the air with words, we simply sit quietly, reducing the internal and external noise to become as still as possible. Communing with God in this form of prayer goes beyond mere words.

These three prayer practices are devotional techniques from the ages but are not the essence of spiritual formation. My friend David Wray helped me understand how we can move toward the goal of transformation by leaning into conversations with God and others. Wray describes the following three ways to invest our lives in transformation.

First, we invest our lives in others. When we enter the Psalms, we can get outside of ourselves and observe the lives of faithful people struggling like we do. Connecting with the joy and heartache of ancient people of faith helps us better connect with the faith journey of others today.

Second, we invest ourselves in spiritual formation and disciplines that shape our lives. Luke Timothy Johnson says Christian universities and seminaries used to center every course on spiritual formation. A shift occurred, however, toward cognition and informational models. There is a hunger and interest in spiritual formation that is growing again. "The specific Christian spirituality is one that is centered on the experience of God as savior through Jesus. In the messianic pattern enacted by Jesus' life and death, we recognize the model for our own lives. In every situation our instinct is to 'look to Jesus' (Heb. 12:2). From the beginning to end the form of spirituality is the imitation of Christ."[3]

Third, a new inner nature forms in us that changes who we are, and that is spiritual transformation. As Richard Foster says, "Christian Spiritual Formation is the continuing process of life and experience through which we are progressively formed, conformed, and transformed into the image of Jesus Christ."[4] We've done fairly well in many churches with the informational part, but we have not done so well with the other parts: being formed in the image of Christ and being transformed into a new person.

God changes us so we can be ready for relationship with him. God shapes us like a ball of clay on a potter's wheel until we're formed into something useful. Like a clay pot fired in a kiln, so God changes us from one degree of his likeness to the next, according to 2 Corinthians 3:18. All of this connects back to the Psalms. When we pray psalms, we invest ourselves in the lives of others by paying attention to voices other than our own. Over time, these voices will show us how to talk back to God. In the process we too will be formed and shaped anew by the words we speak and continue to hear. When our lump of clay is shaped and then refined by fire, we will be transformed into something useful and ready for God to fill with refreshing, living water.

In the following chapters, as we go deeper into the Psalms, we will zero in on the way the Psalms give us fresh voices, courage, and strength for the road ahead.

Reflection

1. Describe your prayers in terms of human growth. In what stage are you right now?

2. What do you think you can do to grow in how you talk back to God?

3. What do you see as the difference between spiritual formation and spiritual transformation?

Action

1. Using the definitions of Spiritual Formation given in this chapter, write your own short definition of Spiritual Formation.

2. Locate one of your favorite Psalms and tell why it is particularly
    meaningful to you.

3. What phrase in this psalm most moves you and makes it your
    favorite?

PART II

VOICES

Chapter 4

VOICING THE UNSPEAKABLE

The famous ballerina Anna Pavlova was once asked,
"When you dance, what are you saying?" Pavlova replied,
"If I could tell you, I wouldn't need to dance."

During my year of pilgrimage in the Psalms, I discovered several powerful values and advantages of praying the Psalms. The first three chapters have served to prepare us for these key discoveries about the Psalms. When we hunger for God, pay attention, and begin to talk back to God, we enter the Psalms with a new way of seeing and hearing. This new orientation to life and God allows us to discover new ways the Psalms can transform our lives.

In the following chapters, we'll go deeper into the function of the Psalms that help us talk back to God in specific ways. Different psalms have different functions: some offer praise, some complain, some call for vengeance, many express lament, and some offer thanksgiving. So as we see how Psalms functioned for ancient Jews and early Christians, we also learn how the Psalms can function in our lives.

What do we discover when we talk back to God using the Psalms? Exactly what blessings can come from praying and praising through the Psalms? The benefits are rich and many. These discoveries have kept me praying, reading, singing, memorizing, and ministering out of the Psalms for many years, and I plan to be doing this the rest of my life. The Psalms supply words and images that name and express tidal waves of emotions when our own words fail us. We've learned already that the Psalms help us pay attention to the hunger for God. The Psalms also help us learn how to talk to God. Not only do they instruct us and show us how to begin talking to God, they also help us speak in new ways that we've feared God may not accept or want to hear.

So the first discovery is that the Psalms give us a voice to speak the unspeakable.

A friend of mine, Mark Abshier, told me about the tragic death of a high school student in his community. He was murdered during a petty robbery. At the funeral, high school students and faculty needed a voice to express what was unspeakable. Mark opened Psalm 29 to them that day. He said this psalm begins with worship that we'd expect in places like church. But the psalmist does not let us stay in church. We go out into the world and experience storms so devastatingly strong that mountains fall and nations tremble. But God is in the storm.

"The psalmist helps us dismantle a hybrid deism that many people hold: the view that God is there but is not near. But the psalmist writes that God is enthroned above the flood. In spite of the flood of tears,

God is near. That's the new orientation that comes at the end of the psalm. Psalm 29:11 says, "The LORD gives strength to his people; the LORD blesses his people with peace." God is there and blesses his people with strength and peace—two things we need in seasons of tragedy. Psalm 29 brought peace and comfort to a lot of people who found themselves in unspeakable pain," Mark said.

The Psalms do not aim to spell things out in propositions or to explain things. The Psalms, after all, are poetry. And poetry gathers up inexpressibly gigantic emotions into sounds and suggestions and images, and launches them in the general direction of expression. This expression goes beyond our minds and resonates with our hearts. It often slips past the defense mechanisms of the brain and infiltrates the whole body and soul—where things too big for words reside. The words of the poems engage soul-deep feelings that cannot be expressed in mere words.

As my friend Jay Scott Embry puts it, "The words on a page seem small, but somehow in music they seem more like the fringes of that thing I see and want to say. For me, this is poetry. For me this is prayer."[1] For the God-hungry, poetry and the music evoked by poetry reach their inspired best in the Psalms.

If worshipers across the centuries could express all they were feeling, they wouldn't need the imagery, the poetry, and the sound of the Psalms. For most of us, rumbling feelings and passions defy our meager vocabulary and bland imagery. Psalmic poetry often identifies and expresses these gargantuan feelings for us.

The Apostle Paul alludes to these intense feelings when he said, "We do not know how to pray as we ought. But the spirit himself intercedes for us with sighs too deep for words" (Romans 8:26). Sometimes words fail us. Our prayers are not poetic. More often for many of us, our prayers are too brisk even to consider the poetry of prayer and imagery of God and to truly empty our feelings before him. Why do we lack this kind of prayer life? Too much noise and not enough reflection. Turning off and tuning out the noise, getting quiet, going into solitude are some of the disciplines that help us enter the Psalms, reflect on the words, and voice the unspeakable. God could be our most loving companion and our audience, but he is often unable to get our attention because of our feverishly maintained noise levels. Flip on the television. Turn up the stereo. Snap on the iPod. We crave noise. "We need it," we say, "to kill the boredom."

My father would often say that boredom was good for kids. In other words, Dad was saying that solitude and silence multiplied by time would cultivate powers of imagination in us. Space between the distractions allows us to ponder the massive, quiet realities around us. When I was a kid, we lived twelve dirt-road miles from town and a mile from the closest neighbors. We couldn't afford gadgets. So, many Saturdays and warm summer afternoons, to "kill boredom," I would pace endlessly over our ranch or find a quiet place in the bushes to sit and imagine. I wrote poems and songs, invented machines, created novels, and amassed fortunes—all in my imagination.

Those early experiences left me with a bent toward reflective thought and an infatuation with words. Also in those quiet days of solitude, I fell in love with storytelling. Best of all, there was time for my mind to wander through the universe and explore thoughts about God. In early childhood, this became my habit.

Even today, much of the imagery through which I communicate was born out of that "boredom" long ago. My father was right. To a tiny degree I identify with the things the Almighty was doing in King David through his loneliness. I imagine David writing psalms out of the reflective habits he learned as a boy shepherd. I believe this is how David's psalms were born.

David's pen recorded the heart music of those days. He wrote and sang his yearnings and reflections about Adonai, the Lord. Three thousand years later, through those psalms we may enter quickly into the secret places of David's soul and on into the presence of God. Of my two favorite psalms, one is attributed to David, the other to the Sons of Korah. One day I would love to hear David and those Sons of Korah sing these songs, from Psalm 63 and 42.

Psalm 63

A psalm of David. When he was in the Desert of Judah.

O God, you are my God,
  earnestly I seek you;
  my soul thirsts for you,
  my body longs for you,
  in a dry and weary land
  where there is no water.
I have seen you in the sanctuary
  and beheld your power and your glory.
Because your love is better than life,
  my lips will glorify you.

I will praise you as long as I live,
>and in your name I will lift up my hands.
My soul will be satisfied as with the richest of foods;
>with singing lips my mouth will praise you.
On my bed I remember you;
>I think of you through the watches of the night.
Because you are my help,
>I sing in the shadow of your wings.
My soul clings to you;
>your right hand upholds me.
They who seek my life will be destroyed;
>they will go down to the depths of the earth.
They will be given over to the sword
>and become food for jackals.
But the king will rejoice in God;
>all who swear by God's name will praise him,
>while the mouths of liars will be silenced.

✦ ✦ ✦ ✦ ✦

Psalm 42

For the director of music. A maskil of the Sons of Korah.
>As the deer pants for streams of water,
>>so my soul pants for you, O God.
>My soul thirsts for God, for the living God.
>>When can I go and meet with God?

My tears have been my food
    day and night,
while men say to me all day long,
    "Where is your God?"
These things I remember
    as I pour out my soul:
how I used to go with the multitude,
    leading the procession to the house of God,
with shouts of joy and thanksgiving
    among the festive throng.
Why are you downcast, O my soul?
    Why so disturbed within me?
Put your hope in God,
    for I will yet praise him,
    my Savior and my God.
My soul is downcast within me;
    therefore I will remember you
from the land of the Jordan,
    the heights of Hermon—from Mount Mizar.
Deep calls to deep
    in the roar of your waterfalls;
all your waves and breakers
    have swept over me.
By day the LORD directs his love,
    at night his song is with me—
    a prayer to the God of my life.

I say to God my Rock,
    "Why have you forgotten me?
Why must I go about mourning,
    oppressed by the enemy?"
My bones suffer mortal agony
    as my foes taunt me,
saying to me all day long,
    "Where is your God?"
Why are you downcast, O my soul?
    Why so disturbed within me?
Put your hope in God,
    for I will yet praise him,
    my Savior and my God.

The Psalms are roadways between the shepherd's lonely heart and the Almighty. Have you ever written a psalm or poem? Many of us were assigned to write poems in school, but few people these days write poems or psalms by choice. Reflection and creativity are incredibly difficult in a world constantly reverberating with noise and motion. No exalted vision emerges from the heavens when our consciousness is a constant blur.

Occasionally we meet genuinely reflective people, however, and we are drawn to them. One time when my friend Landon Saunders was speaking to a gathering, another friend of mine, Glenn Owen, leaned over to me and said, "The man's got the glow." I knew what he meant and I agree! People like Landon Saunders have about them a glow from the throne room of God. They are people who pursue God.

I can tell when someone lives in the Psalms, in Scripture, and in pursuit of God. We envy them with a "good envy"! They inspire us, convict us, and soothe us. Such hearts God uses best—hearts grown sensitive to the things of God through quietness.

Of course, this kind of help will not come out of a superficial reading of the Psalms—not even from the first few thoughtful readings. But given time, the Psalms begin to voice the unspeakable for us. Surely this is one huge reason God gave them to us.

But when I try to speak the unspeakable, I don't always have the vocabulary of prayer. I get bogged down using the few prayer phrases I learned in early years of faith and from hearing others pray. Perhaps you've experienced this too, so you might identify with these "prayer blockers." One of my "prayer blockers" that causes me to drift to the shallows is when I use those same old stale phrases. If I am experiencing big things for which I have no vocabulary, I am tempted simply to ignore them and pray only within the limits of my own bland vocabulary.

But the Psalms can keep my prayers in deeper places. Because Psalms put us in touch with the unspeakable, our connection with God grows deeper and broader and stronger through them. When we read the Psalms, the words are sometimes unclear but we sense a deeper meaning. For example, some of the language in Psalm 42 is straightforward. "As a deer pants for water, so my soul pants for you, Oh God." Questions such as, "When can I go and meet with God?" express powerful feelings in a clear way. So when reading the Psalms, start with words like these you can understand. After that, move on to words that seem to be expressing some deeper longing. Sometimes we have to start with the obviously clear things and move deeper to things we are less conscious of in our lives. That's how the Psalms work and how our lives work.

As we move further into the Psalm 42, we are not sure what the words mean when the psalmist says, "from the land of the Jordan, from Mount Mizar." We feel a mood, but we are not sure what the language means if taken literally.

Still further into Psalm 42, the words become weighty and we wonder what they mean. "Deep calls to deep in the roar of your waterfalls. All your waves and breakers have swept over me." The language seems to escape logical understanding. Yet, when we read these words, we too may feel the deep calling to deep in a way we can't quite express. The psalm begins to help us bring out something that is unspeakable. We don't know what it means, yet we do know what it means—though we cannot explain it in words.

Poetry is poetry and will not be tamed and bridled by exegesis or analysis. The same could be said of the words, "My bones suffer mortal agony, while men say to me all day long, 'Where is your God?'" Now really? Mortal agony? How? Yet the phrase strikes an inexplicable yet very real chord deep within us.

Some of the Psalms say what we are experiencing but in language we don't understand. We don't know. Yet we know. Sometimes this comes through in the very rhythm of the psalm. For example, Psalm 131 repeats a phrase, "But I have stilled and quieted my soul; like a weaned child with its mother, like a weaned child is my soul within me." The phrase has some meaning on the face of it. But the rhythm of the repetition picks up on something inexplicable within us. We know what we are experiencing, but we also get the sense that we don't know how to say what these rhythmic phrases stir within us.

Another example of this phenomenon appears in Psalm 130: "My soul waits for the Lord more than watchmen wait for the morning, more than watchmen wait for the morning." While these phrases make some metaphorical sense on the surface, at the same time they get their fingernails under the edge of things we feel strongly but cannot explain.

In other cases, however, the Psalms take flight into lavish metaphorical language that resonates with our spirits but again defies explanation. One example of this is Psalm 23, the most familiar psalm of all. In spite of its familiarity, we don't know for sure exactly what Psalm 23 is saying. But we know that Psalm 23 resonates with our hearts.

We have many interpretations of Psalm 23. Is it an assurance psalm? Is it prophetic? Is Psalm 23 a word about obedience? Does it speak to grief? Certainly this is one of the most quoted psalms at graveside services. Is the psalm for private reflection or to be read in the "midst of the congregation"? And what on earth is the "table spread in the wilderness" and how are the enemies present?

Perhaps Psalm 23 is all of the above and much more. Actually, I think the wide spectrum of interpretation is not because Psalm 23 is vague, but because the psalm is so incredibly rich with meaning. Heraclitus said, "No one can step into the same river twice." And no one can "step into the same psalm twice." Psalm 23 is fresh and new with every reading because it catches up with us in different situations or moods and sometimes hits us right in that unspeakable place in our soul, that "sweet spot" for the Psalms. So maybe God intended Psalm

23 to speak a current message depending on where we are when it catches up with us!

In spite of its shroud of mystery, Psalm 23 says to us, on levels we cannot express for ourselves, that God is all we need and that God is always with us—no matter what.

Psalm 84 is another familiar psalm that says so much more than what we read on the surface. This is a song of a pilgrim on the way to Jerusalem. It praises the Temple as the "lovely dwelling place of God"—a presence for which the pilgrim's "soul yearns and faints" and for which his or her "heart and flesh cry out." And within whose courts, "one day is better than a thousand elsewhere." Yet it is not really about a temple and its courts—particularly not for us psalm singers all these centuries later. It is about something unspeakably more. It touches a longing so large and so deep that it can only be voiced in poetic metaphor.

The Psalms help us get close to the places in our hearts we cannot tell about in mere words. Through metaphors and word pictures, the rich psalm language opens our ears to hear from God and our voices to speak to God. Again, we cannot describe what every phrase of a psalm is saying, but we "know" what we know. We experience the voice of the unspeakable when we hear these psalms.

The Psalms are so rich and varied that we'll look deeper at their variety chapter by chapter. Likewise, the Reflections and Actions at the end of the book are also designed for you to explore the various benefits of the Psalms, and to bring them into your own prayers as you encounter God.

Reflection

1. Discuss a time when you felt unable to speak the unspeakable?

2. What psalm most speaks the unspeakable to you today and why?

3. Why do you suppose so few of us have ever written a psalm?

4. If you wrote a psalm of your own, what unspeakable thing would it be about?

Action

1. Choose a particular psalm that helps you explore the unspeakable.

2. Read through the psalm slowly, reflectively, aloud at first just to get an overview.

3. Pray through the psalm carefully, making your prayer personal.

4. Pray the psalm aloud again, this time on behalf of others.

5. Finally, pray the psalm aloud in sheer adoration of God—listening for his voice and surrendering to his will.

6. Don't stop praying when the psalm ends. Go on from there and let that psalm be a springboard for praying about the current issues and persons that psalm has brought to your heart. Let the mood and the content of the psalm shape your prayer focus for the day.

Chapter 5

EXPLORING THE UNTHINKABLE

"But the soul that perseveres through the dark night
comes to the dawn of a new day."

—Simon Chan[1]

In the previous chapter we saw how Psalms help us voice the unspeakable. The Psalms also help us explore the unthinkable. How can we voice anger, anxiety, our deepest fears and darkest thoughts to God? Psalms drill down into the marrow, getting to the core issues of life.

Through the Psalms, God provides therapy for these intense and sometimes painful issues. They help put us in touch with buried issues. I have discovered that the Psalms often surface enormously significant feelings I did not even know were there. Or even more to the point, the Psalms unearth things we desperately need to face—wounds that will not be healed unless they are surfaced and dealt with carefully. We know they are in there somewhere, but we don't want to deal with them. They seem too painful or too frightening or too threatening to face.

As we move through the Psalms, however, some of them take us into that unthinkable emotional geography we might otherwise avoid. They lead us to process painful feelings we might otherwise stuff down inside. This processing releases healing into our souls.

Robert Duvall plays a tent evangelist in the movie, "The Apostle." One scene depicts a great example of talking back to God. Duvall, the preacher, is raging in an upstairs room at his mother's house. He had just discovered that his wife was having an affair with the youth minister. He shouts his prayers to God, but his eyes are open and blazing. He shakes his fist toward the ceiling.

"They stole my church, stole my wife! If you won't give me back my wife, give me peace!" he shouts.

As he paces the floor and flails his arms, he presses God further.

"Give it to me, give it to me, give it to me! Give me peace!"

But he doesn't stop there. Duvall's Apostle gets downright angry at God and doesn't hold back.

"I'm confused, I'm mad. I love you, Lord, but I'm mad at you! I know I'm a sinner, once in a while—womanizer—but I'm your servant. What do you want me to do? Should I lay hands on myself? What do you want me to do?"

The scene is intense and full of humanity. Yet it also portrays a profoundly rich theology of prayer. The Psalms give us permission to let God know when we feel abandoned or mistreated.

Even Jesus himself gives us permission to pour out our grievances to God, to express negative feelings of being abandoned by God.

The cross is not the only place we see Jesus praying lament or protest prayers. When Jesus had come back to Jerusalem during the Passover, he went with his disciples to the Garden of Gethsemane, just across from a city gate. In the garden Jesus pleaded with his Father, "Let this cup pass from me." He was talking about the cup of suffering on the cross. In essence, he was asking God to find another way. He went through the sense of abandonment one feels when our prayers do not seem to be answered. This becomes crystal clear when Jesus, hanging on the cross in the gathering darkness, cries out with a loud voice, "My God, my God, why have you forsaken me?" At that horrendous moment, Jesus was praying the words from Psalm 22:1-3:

My God, my God, why have you forsaken me?
Why are you so far from saving me,
so far from the words of my groaning?
O my God, I cry out by day, but you do not answer,
by night, and am not silent.
Yet you are enthroned as the Holy One;
you are the praise of Israel.

Many people wrestle with those words of Jesus on the cross. How can God the Father forsake God the Son? We often focus on such abstract theological questions, when what appears to be taking place has more to do with the relationship between Christ and the Father. What can we learn about God by overhearing this incredibly personal expression from Christ on the cross, "My God, my God, why have you forsaken me?" What we are hearing from Jesus is a prayer of deep lament. And in these moments, with these words, Christ did a great service to the world. These words, welling up out of his deepest agony, give us permission to cry out as well.

Our "make me happy" culture programs us to avoid painful or negative feelings. But serious downsides come with this kind of avoidance. Mental health professionals have long since discovered that swallowed painful feelings—such as anger, fear, and shame—usually produce even more negative consequences. These feelings frequently come out in some destructive form, such as clinical depression, substance abuse, or sexual acting out.

The Psalms are not about stuffing or denying buried issues. Perhaps this is why looking at the Psalms—or any Scripture—from a moralistic or legalistic perspective drains the life and pursuit of God out of those coming from these perspectives. Psalms are not to-do lists or even not-to-do lists for entrance into heaven. Neither are the Psalms pure venting. Venting alone—particularly the kind that diminishes other people or God—can make our problems seem larger than life and spread the stress to others. Rather than stuffing or venting, we're instructed to pray to God. The Psalms give us a praying voice that is not stuffing, not venting, but something much more. Reading, praying, singing, memorizing, and ministering the Psalms gives us an emotional and spiritual health that helps us deal with the dark side of our hearts. God knew this before the Psalms were ever voiced.

In Psalm 32:3-4 the psalmist says,

When I kept silent,
　　my bones wasted away
　　through my groaning all day long.

For day and night
    your hand was heavy upon me;
    my strength was sapped
    as in the heat of summer.

But then comes the therapy and redemption in the next verse:

Then I acknowledged my sin to you
    and did not cover up my iniquity.
I said, "I will confess
    my transgressions to the LORD"—
and you forgave
    the guilt of my sin.
Therefore let everyone who is godly pray to you
    while you may be found;
surely when the mighty waters rise,
    they will not reach him.
You are my hiding place;
    you will protect me from trouble
    and surround me with songs of deliverance.

Apparently one reason God gave us the Psalms is to help us unearth these kinds of feelings and deal with them. Approximately seventy percent of the recorded Psalms in the Old Testament are psalms of complaint, lament, or imprecation, which means vengeance.

By praying these Psalms we lay our stuff honestly at God's feet. God is big enough to let us beat on his chest. We need not pretend we have no negative, angry feelings toward God. In fact, he already knows we have those feelings anyway. Rather, we have both permission and language to open our hearts and show rage, disappointment, and anger at God. In fact, Psalm 13 does just that:

How long, O LORD? Will you forget me forever?
How long will you hide your face from me?
How long must I wrestle with my thoughts
and every day have sorrow in my heart?
How long will my enemy triumph over me?

As we read and pray and sing *all* the variety of the Psalms—laments as well as praises, imprecatory psalms as well as warm, fuzzy ones and bright "Halleluiahs"—they will eventually take us into that emotional geography we might otherwise try to avoid. They lead us to process painful feelings we might otherwise just stuff down inside.

A Christian woman, struggling with doubts and darkness, confided, "I can hardly stand to go to church. Not that I don't want to worship God or be around his people. It's just that everything sounds so damn *positive*. They sing bright songs, preach upbeat messages, and smile so much—and seem to ignore the pain that must be sitting in those pews. It makes me feel so outside of everything there, so disconnected." This woman eloquently raised a red flag over the marketing mindset invading some contemporary churches. Sometimes the motto seems to be, "Don't talk about negative stuff at church. That won't attract crowds. Let's bring 'em in. Pump 'em up. And send 'em out grinning."

For years I have advocated praise teams to help lead us in worship. I still do, of course, but I have been wondering if we don't also need "lament teams" sometimes. Sunday after Sunday people show up and sit in the pews in some state of real lament. When we sing songs of lament, we recognize this. Remember, these make up seventy percent of the Psalms yet are most often ignored in Christian worship. To keep the mood in our assemblies upbeat, we sometimes even pillage bright phrases from psalms of lament, and we turn them into upbeat praise choruses.

For example, the words "As a deer pants for the water, so my soul longs after you" are lifted from the anguish of Psalm 42 and spliced into a warm adoring popular praise song. The real point of Psalm 42 doesn't sing well in a praise chorus, so it is left behind. Listen to some of the lament in Psalm 42:3, 5:

> My tears have been my food day and night,
> while men say to me all day long,
>> "Where is your God?"
>
> Why are you downcast, O my soul?
>> Why so disturbed within me?

The point is that the happy tunes we sing often don't match the words of the Psalms. This is merely one example of bright phrases stripped from the heart of a lament psalm.

Of course, even most psalms of lament end with a triumphal note of hope—with one glaring exception: Psalm 88. To get the feel of what I am talking about, please take a few moments to read Psalm 88 aloud, thoughtfully and reflectively.

> O LORD, the God who saves me,day and night I cry out
>> before you.

May my prayer come before you;
 turn your ear to my cry.
For my soul is full of trouble
 and my life draws near the grave.
I am counted among those who go down to the pit;
 I am like a man without strength.
I am set apart with the dead,
 like the slain who lie in the grave,
whom you remember no more,
 who are cut off from your care.
You have put me in the lowest pit,
 in the darkest depths.
Your wrath lies heavily upon me;
 you have overwhelmed me with all your waves.
  Selah
You have taken from me my closest friends
 and have made me repulsive to them.
I am confined and cannot escape;
 my eyes are dim with grief.
I call to you, O LORD, every day;
 I spread out my hands to you.
Do you show your wonders to the dead?
 Do those who are dead rise up and praise you?
  Selah
Is your love declared in the grave,
 your faithfulness in Destruction?

Are your wonders known in the place of darkness,
 or your righteous deeds in the land of oblivion?
But I cry to you for help, O LORD;
 in the morning my prayer comes before you.
Why, O LORD, do you reject me
 and hide your face from me?
From my youth I have been afflicted and close to death;
 I have suffered your terrors and am in despair.
Your wrath has swept over me;
 your terrors have destroyed me.
All day long they surround me like a flood;
 they have completely engulfed me.
You have taken my companions and loved ones from me;
 the darkness is my closest friend.

See what I mean? The dark Psalm 88 seems to contain no hope and ends on a dismal note: "The darkness is my closest friend."

I read Psalm 88 to the woman who hated going to her church that never offered a chance to lament. After I finished reading this lament psalm, she sat quietly a long time. Finally, she looked up and blurted out, "Why don't we plan a worship assembly around *this* psalm? We are always a 'praise team.' Why not for once a 'lament team'? I'll bet some Sundays nearly everyone in the place would resonate with it."

A surprising number of people in your church might be helped enormously if some Sunday your worship leaders planned an entire worship assembly around Psalm 88. You might be surprised as well to find out that God would be pleased with a lament service. God knows our needs and our long periods of darkness. That is why he allowed and left those dark psalms in the Bible. I need them. We need them. Our churches need them, too.

Of course, the same could be said of our private and personal prayers. We will find it to be therapeutic and freeing when we go into the dark corners of our hearts. And moving slowly, deliberately through the Psalms will inevitably take us there.

So the Psalms supply language and permission to express our negative feelings. This, in turn, offers therapy—and ultimately healing. Psalms help us voice the unspeakable and uncomfortable and give us permission to pour out our hearts to God. And who better to hear us than the God who knows our grief and welcomes our lament?

So, getting into the Psalms becomes a challenge in several new ways. First, praying a psalm may seem challenging in the beginning because you are entering new emotional territory or trying a new form of prayer. Second, when you become more comfortable with reading and praying the Psalms, the challenge becomes getting to those uncomfortable and unspeakable places in your life. Third, the Psalms then lead us to new challenges in praying and crying out for others.

If your first experiences in the Psalms don't do anything for you, stay with it and continue to move to new psalms. In these early stages you are learning some mechanics of how to read and pray the Psalms, so expect to feel a bit awkward. You may not get to the deeper levels right at first. This is fairly normal. Don't quit. We have heard of Ken Blanchard's "one-minute manager," but there is no such thing as a "one-minute contemplative"!

Stay with the psalm reading and praying exercises, and later move into singing and even memorizing psalms. Trust the process. After all, just as one nutritious meal won't make an undernourished person healthy, neither will one psalm instantly cure spiritual scurvy.

True, my specific way of praying and singing the psalms may not be armor that fits you over the long haul. But it is a starting place, a pump primer. And when you get drawn into the Psalms as the core of your worship life, you will likely find a specific technique for praying the Psalms that fits you better—it will become your sling and stone.

Reflection

1. How have you experienced or not experienced healing through the "therapy of a psalm"?

2. What psalms speak best to your inner feelings of pain, shame, anger, or guilt?

3. What particular lines are most meaningful to you and why?

Action

Pick a psalm that helps you explore the uncomfortable. Consider one of the following: Psalm 2, 42, 51, 88, 13.

1. *Read* through a psalm of lament or an imprecatory psalm—reflectively, slowly, aloud.

2. Then *pray* through it aloud carefully—in the first person, making it your own prayer of lament.

3. Then pray through that psalm aloud again, on behalf of others who are in pain, in the second person.

4. And finally pray the psalm in sheer adoration of God—grateful for his healing—listening for his voice—surrendering to his will.

5. But don't stop praying when the psalm ends. Go on from there to pray about the current issues and persons that psalm has brought to your heart. Let the psalm shape your prayer focus for the day.

PART III

HELPS

Chapter 6

KEEPING IT REAL

You do not have, because you do not ask God. When you ask,
you do not receive, because you ask with wrong motives,
that you may spend what you get on your pleasures.

—James 4:2b-3

So far we've been on a pathway of approaching God through the Psalms. Before we go further up the path, let's stop, turn, and look back down the trail at some milestones we have passed.

We acknowledged that a healthy, disciplined worship life is very difficult for most of us to sustain in the long term. A good deal of the advice we get does not work for long. Then we boldly suggested a secret to the life of prayer: The Psalms can teach us to pray. In fact, the best time-tested practice of great faith warriors for three thousand years is simply praying and singing psalms.

We then began exploring the benefits of pursuing God by praying, singing, and memorizing the Psalms. First, we noted that the Psalms help us *voice* the unspeakable. The Psalms give our hearts a voice where we often can't find the words to speak. Second, the Psalms help us *explore* the unthinkable. The Psalms are full of lament, and simply taking these at face value is something our culture finds difficult, but when we take in these psalms of lament, they give us a kind of therapy that leads to healing.

Now, let's move on to a third benefit that can come from the Psalms. *Praying the Psalms keeps our prayer topics fresh and connected to real life.* The topic and focus keep changing from psalm to psalm, raising fresh prayers with each new psalm we pray. Thus, praying through the Psalms leads us into a wide range of prayer subjects and emotions. In other words, the Psalms bounce us out of our narrow self-focused prayers. What is more, a prayer that begins with a psalm usually moves us beyond the ancient content of the psalm itself and into contemporary issues. So the benefit of fresh prayer topics from the Psalms is that they keep us connected to real life.

A man was once offered a choice: to keep living his life with all its heartache and suffering; or to have a perfect life with none of that pain. Which would he choose? The man thought a while and realized he wouldn't want to live a life where everything was perfect all the time—it seemed boring.

"I'll take the perfect life," he said, "but everything would be like it is now—only my furnace would work."

Our lives are certainly punctuated by good times and bad—the Psalms account for the paradoxes of life. We all experience emotionally dry times—and who would expect pouring rain in these desert days? A skeptical view would see only the desert. A rosy view sees only the fresh water pools and ignores suffering. The Psalms show us both the desert and the pools. No matter how far along the journey, I keep returning to pools of autumn rain in the Valley of Baca. Those pools are more than mirages that trick us or entice us into staying the course in life so we can consume more and be consumed by the trials of life. The Psalms are these pools. These pools refresh us and keep us from hallucinating about our lives. The Psalms keep our prayers fresh, and this connects us to reality. God is reality. Our world is full of illusions that fool us into believing God is only to be found at the end of the journey, in heaven.

But God is here right now. And learning to talk back to God— to voice the unspeakable and pray the unthinkable—connects our daily experience with the reality of God. The pools along the journey reflect God's joy we receive along the way. As Michael Card's song says so beautifully:

There is a joy in the journey
There's a life you can love on the way
There is a wonder and wildness to life
And freedom for those who obey.

The Psalms provide us with pools of fresh water along our journey, particularly for those times when the journey seems most dry and hopeless. The Psalms offer a wide variety of emotion and life experiences, and that matches how we live. We need this variety in order to keep it real and connected to the way we experience life.

For example, contrast the tone and topic of Psalm 88 with Psalm 100. On the one hand, Psalm 88 is full of utter despair. Psalm 100, on the other hand, is full of ecstatic praise. In Psalm 88 we hear the psalmist saying, "Darkness is my only friend." In Psalm 100, the psalm-ist says, "Shout for joy to the Lord, all the earth."

A second example is two contrasting psalms that appear side by side. In fact, these two psalms may originally have been one. The two Psalms are 22 and 23. Psalm 22 speaks of the agony of feeling aban-doned by God. The words, "My God, my God why have you forsaken me" are some of the words Jesus spoke on the cross. Then Psalm 23 is about the warm tender presence of God, our shepherd, who "makes us lie down in green pastures and leads us beside still waters." The prayers arising from a day of prayer from Psalm 22 would be totally different from a day of prayer shaped by Psalm 23.

Not only does praying through the Psalms keep expanding our range of prayer topics, but praying this way can also deepen and broad-en the meaning and purpose of prayer, moving our prayers beyond pure petition or prayer requests.

The prayer practices in church Bible classes and small group gath-erings often go something like this:

Leader: Any prayer requests?

Talkative Attendee: I have a prayer request. My Aunt Sally had a heart attack. Well, she thinks she did, but she's thought that before and it turned out to be heartburn. They took her to the ER and . . . .

Man in a suit: I'm really not happy at my job. I really need a raise or I'm changing jobs. I'd like your prayers that I can either get a better paying job or a raise.

Woman in a flowered dress: My friend and I are going on a cruise! But I've never been out of the country, so with all that's happening in the world, I want to ask for your prayers for a safe trip.

The leader typically chooses someone to say the prayer and to remember each request specifically. The prayer is usually a spontaneous "please, God" prayer—a petition prayer for all the requests that were made.

Of course God is interested in Aunt Sally, in our safety, our marriages, and our journeys. And it pleases God when we "lay all our requests before him." Even listening to the concerns of others is therapeutic for all and helps us break out of ourselves. And petition is not bad either—even the Psalms can be used for petition prayers for others.

Petition on behalf of others is a part of faithful prayer. James 4:2b-3 calls us to ask God to fill our needs. "You do not have, because you do not ask God. When you ask, you do not receive, because you ask with wrong motives, that you may spend what you get on your pleasures" (James 4:2b-3). The problem is petitioning alone with little faithful acknowledgement of God's provision in the first place. The problem James addresses is wrong motives—constantly praying for God to make our lives better so we can prosper without really pursuing the heart of God in relationship. We seek his hand of blessing but not his face in relationship.

Yes, Jesus tells us to "seek, knock, and ask." The problem is not petition itself. The Psalms certainly offer petitions, some nearly demanding God to act on an individual's or group's behalf. Yet in the Psalms, personal petition is *just one small piece* of the possibilities in potent prayer. Sure, the Psalms include many requests and petitions of God. But these take us far beyond mere begging for God to make our lives more convenient.

The Psalms remind us of God's benefits and blessings in a fresh way each day. For example, Psalm 103:2-5 powerfully calls us out of ourselves and to recall the benefits and blessings from the Lord.

Praise the LORD, O my soul,
　　and forget not all his benefits
who forgives all your sins
　　and heals all your diseases,
who redeems your life from the pit
　　and crowns you with love and compassion,
who satisfies your desires with good things
　　so that your youth is renewed like the eagle's.

When we move methodically through the Psalms, amazing things happen.

They have us listening to God.

They have us praising God.

Thanking God.

Exploring our own souls.

Confessing our sins to God.

Blessing other people.

Empathizing with the pain of others.

Spewing our anger at God.

Recalling God's goodness.

Asking God questions.

Seeking God's face.

Being awestruck at his majesty.

Trembling before his holiness.

Basking in his love.

Praying the Psalms vastly broadens and deeply enriches our understanding of the purposes and power of prayer. Our prayer life grows fresher, more meaningful, and our relationship with God grows deeper as the Psalms teach us to praise and honor God.

The Psalms move through a rich and ever-changing landscape of emotions and issues. Our prayers will remain fresh if we choose a psalm that launches us into our daily routine with new themes of worship, lament, thanksgiving, or reflection on God's mighty works. Remember, once we have prayed our psalm aloud three times—the first time to get a feel for the psalm, the second time on behalf of ourselves, and the third time on behalf of someone else—we don't stop praying when the psalm ends; rather we let its theme shape the rest of our prayer for the day.

Now let's note just a few examples of the variety of topics suggested by the Psalms. Even in the beginning of the book of Psalms, each psalm leads us through rapidly changing terrain. Psalm 1 blesses the person who does not hobnob with the ungodly but rather "delights in the law [the instruction] of the Lord and meditates on it day and night." In time that person becomes as fruitful as a "tree planted by streams of water." All his or her "ways will prosper." He or she will "stand in judgment" and "in the assembly of the righteous" and will be known by the Lord, in contrast to "the way of the ungodly" who will "perish."

The psalm is about the blessedness of seeking God and the prayer theme for the day out of Psalm 1 can center on fruitfulness and prosperity for which we praise God alone. The theme of Psalm 1 also suggests prayer for "ungodly" friends who are miserable and perishing.

Psalm 3 shifts direction abruptly. "O LORD, how many are my foes! How many rise up against me! Many are saying of me, 'God will not deliver him.'" This is a prayer of desperation over all the "foes" that surround us—whether they are real live enemies or sins that plague our lives, an illness, or bankruptcy. This theme of desperation in the "face of surrounding foes" might shape the rest of our prayer for the day we are in Psalm 3.

Psalm 5 shifts directions again. Here David asks God to listen: "Give ear to my words, O Lord, consider my sighing." He not only addresses God directly but reminds God of his greatness and mercy. He even tells God what he is not. "You are not a God who takes pleasure in evil." This psalm paints great contrasts between those who come to God by his great mercy and those who have rebelled against God. "For surely, O Lord, you bless the righteous; you surround them with your favor as with a shield."

Psalm 8 is a hymn of praise and adoration of the Creator. "O LORD, our Lord, how majestic is your name in all the earth! You have set your glory above the heavens." But Psalm 8 is also praise to the one whose fingers have made the moon and stars, yet who cares for human beings so that we have been exalted above the heavenly beings, and given dominion over created beings, "flocks and herds . . . birds of the air . . . the fish of the sea, all that swim the paths of the sea." The psalm then ends with another burst of exuberant praise, matching the one with which it began. "O LORD, our Lord, how majestic is your name in all the earth!" This psalm sets a fresh and overwhelmingly positive tone for prayer.

So Psalms 1, 3, 5, and 8 radically change the subject four times in the first week of praying through the book of Psalms. And this is with 142 psalms to go.

Flying over the Psalms at thirty-five thousand feet, we can see general shifts of major themes, styles, and authors. The Psalms are divided into five books or collections of psalms. Most Bibles show these divisions, but ancient texts separate them differently. It appears that each of the five collections may have been used in different Jewish worshiping communities for centuries then collected into the book of Psalms as we know it today.

Book one spans Psalms 1-41 which were mostly composed by or attributed to David. They express much of David's view of God's glory, power over enemies, and great mercy for sinners. Jehovah, translated Lord, is used throughout this section of the Psalms. There's no way to adequately summarize the variety in the collections, but Psalms 1-41 sets the scene for the relationship between God and humanity. David knows, as in Psalm 7, that God is his refuge, the one who will save and deliver him from enemies and sin. But he also honestly wonders aloud why God seems distant in times of trouble, as in Psalm 10. The worldview set up in these psalms is that God is the Lord and we are not. As David asks in Psalm 8, "What is man that you are mindful of him?" Still, David says in Psalm 41 that God does deliver in times of trouble, helps the weak and the sinner, and triumphs over enemies.

Book two covers Psalms 42-72 where psalmists address El or Elohim, which is translated "God." Most of these psalms are attributed to David, though Solomon wrote one and the Sons of Korah wrote several others. Book two exhibits a palpable sense of Israel's exile and ruin and issues a call for God's deliverance. Psalm 42 sets the scene with word pictures of a desert where there is no water, where deep calls to deep and the soul is downcast. Then Psalm 46 raises a confident cry of God's strength and ever-present help in times of trouble, inviting worshipers to "come and see the works of the Lord." The call is to be still and know that he is God.

The third book runs from Psalms 73-89 and Asaph appears to have written most of them. The divine title used is "God." Most of the psalms were written by priests and sung in temple choirs. The psalm that set the scene for *Talking Back to God*, Psalm 84, is a good example of the style and theme of this third section. Here the psalmist exclaims, "How lovely is your dwelling place, O Lord Almighty!" The basis for this praise is God's faithfulness; he has kept his covenant. The last psalm in this section—Psalm 89—exults in God's faithfulness to the covenant of love he established with Israel. This section is not without honest questioning, lament, and doubt: it ends with the psalmist asking, "How long, O Lord? Will you hide yourself forever?" The cry is for God again to show the great love he showed to David. Each of the books ends with a final "Amen." Book three ends with a double Amen: "Praise be to the Lord forever. Amen and Amen."

Book four is another short section spanning Psalms 90-106. Psalm 90 opens with a psalm attributed to Moses where he says, "Who knows the power of your anger? For your wrath is as great as the fear that is due you." Yet he calls upon God to have favor on the people and establish the work of their hands. The phrase is repeated and emphatic: "May the favor of the Lord our God rest upon us; establish the work of our hands for us—yes, establish the work of our hands." Doxology ends this section as it does each of the sections: "Praise be to the Lord, the God of Israel, from everlasting to everlasting. Let all the people say, Amen!" (106).

Book five spans Psalm 107-150 and the major theme is thanksgiving. This section includes what are called "Psalms of Ascent" that lead God's people to worship in the temple. The most perfect sacrifice is faithful obedience in the lives of people who then show God praise and thanksgiving. Of the forty-four psalms in this book, fifteen are attributed to David, one to Solomon, and most have no attribution. Jehovah, translated "Lord," is used in this fifth book. This collection includes the memory of exile, as in Psalm 137: "By the Rivers of Babylon we sat down and wept when we remembered Zion." While lament and cries to the Lord are included—"I cry aloud to the Lord; I lift up my voice to the Lord for mercy" (142:1), book five is known for psalms that begin and end with "Praise the Lord." Book five—and the whole book of Psalms—ends with a word of celebration: "Let everything that has breath praise the Lord. Praise the Lord" (150).

So there is an incredible amount of variety throughout the book of Psalms. This variety helps bring variety and depth to our prayer life. Praying through the Psalms gets us out of our ruts and brings steady freshness to our daily prayers. They can expand our shrinking prayer lists, and keep us from prayer focused too heavily on petition. The Psalms give us prayer themes that we often find difficult to come up with ourselves. Talking back to God about what we experience in his creation, whether good or bad, calls for broader language that the Psalms supply.

The Reflection and Action section at the end of each chapter is intended to help you or your group go deeper into praying the Psalms. Each of us learns differently, so if the exercises don't suit your needs, skip over them as you read. The strongest encouragement is to get into the Psalms—first reading one psalm a day, then gradually reading more and letting them soak into your consciousness. As you go through each day, you may be surprised at the fresh variety of phrases that come to mind from the psalms when you begin praying them.

Reflection

1. What different real life situations come to mind as you read through this list of topics in the Psalms?
   Listening to God. Praising God. Thanking God. Exploring our own souls. Confessing our sins to God. Blessing other people. Empathizing with the pain of others. Spewing our anger at God. Recalling God's goodness. Asking God questions. Seeking God's face. Being awestruck at his majesty. Trembling before his holiness. Basking in his love.

2. Think or talk about a time when you have felt stuck in a monotonous prayer rut—same old topics, same old words. What did you do about it?

Action

1. Make a list of topics on which your prayers have most often felt "stuck."

2. Read back through the list of themes in the Reflection section above and write beside each one a real-life, immediate prayer situation each of them raises.

3. Stop now and pray for God to lead you into more variety and freshness in your prayer life.

4. Write a sentence or two describing how praying the Psalms could help lift you out of your prayer rut.

Chapter 7

BREAKING OUT OF
OURSELVES

Jesus came to define the Kingdom of God. Jesus came
to show what it means when the Lord reigns . . . . .

—Josh Graves, The Feast

W hen I married Carolyn, I did not marry her to get her car, or
her house, or her money, or her prestige. I married her because I wanted her—just her and no one else. The reward of marrying
Carolyn is Carolyn. And half a century later, the more I have of her, the
more I want.

Just like a marriage where the reward is each other, so the reward
of serving God is God. That's why the age-old question, "What's in it
for me?" is wrong-headed and wrong-hearted. Worship is about God.
It is not about what we can get out of it.

The Psalms function not only to help us speak the unspeakable
and uncomfortable but also to keep our prayers fresh, which leads

us to break out of ourselves. Rather than asking, almost as a demand, "God, give us a good day," we ask, "God, who is like you in all the universe?" The Psalms break us out of our bondage of selfish desires that wage battle against our desire to pursue God. *By the simple act of noticing people around us in prayer, we break out of ourselves.*

To emphasize breaking out of ourselves, we're going to break away from the Psalms on a brief detour, going backward to the beginning of God's story and forward into the Gospels.

From the beginning, God has continually turned us back to himself, reminding us that our lives are not our own. Our lives are for him. The prayers we pray shape whether we live for ourselves or for God. Jesus taught his disciples a simple prayer that we continue speaking today. The model prayer of Jesus—traditionally called "The Lord's Prayer"—teaches us something about praying the Psalms. Many Christians believe the whole gospel story simply drives toward the cross and the atonement of Christ. These are vitally important to the gospel story, but Matthew's Gospel drives toward a larger picture than the atonement and going to heaven when we die. Rather, what we see in the Gospels is Jesus coming to incarnate the new kingdom where the sick are healed, the aliens are taken care of, and the weak are not left behind.

Matthew, the writer of the first Gospel of Christ, quotes Jesus' prayer to say something big about the good news of the kingdom of God. For Matthew, the kingdom is the reign of God—everywhere and in all things. And he fills out the kingdom mission as caring for those who suffer and hurt: caring for the sick, visiting the imprisoned, feeding the hungry, clothing the naked, and embracing the homeless.

Matthew's Gospel climaxes with Jesus claiming a cosmic, all encompassing reign. He says, "*All* authority in heaven and on earth has been given to me."

So, where are the Psalms in all this? Step back and look at the Lord's Prayer from a wider point of view. Could the Lord's Prayer actually summarize what it means to pray the Psalms?

This prayer that begins with the words, "Your kingdom come, your will be done on earth as it is in heaven," is consistent with Matthew's kingdom message. Even the postscript that seems to have been added in later years—"For yours is the kingdom and the power and the glory for ever and ever"—is consistent with Matthew's kingdom message.

The Kingdom. God rules all, and he wants us to allow him to reign in our lives.

The Power. He alone has the power to bring about his will, but he will not force it upon us.

The Glory. Since God rules all, and since he supplies all the power to follow his reign, so he alone deserves all the glory.

A friend of mine summarizes the Lord's Prayer like this:

Help.

Wow.

Thank you.

And the Lord's Prayer hits the mark in summarizing the Psalms. The Psalms definitely get us out of ourselves, taking us on a journey everyday from the petition ("Help!"), to praise ("Wow!"), to gratitude that imitates the heart of God ("Thank you!").

Sometimes we get stuck in the "Help!" part of prayer. Moving through the Psalms often pulls us out of our narrow band of self-consumed prayer and into the experiences of people around us. The Psalms move through a variety of emotions and topics that change our prayer topics from psalm to psalm. And many of them open real connection with needs beyond our own and this energizes our prayers. When you read a psalm aloud, especially in a gathering, it may not directly connect with what you are feeling at the time. But it may connect you with the very real and current feelings of someone else in your circle.

In his book *Answering God*, Eugene Peterson describes how the Psalms take us into the lives of others:

> I open the Psalms . . . and find myself in the place of prayer, ready to pray. I look around and see thirty other men and women . . . from thirty different places, reared in thirty different homes and in the past few hours have experienced thirty different combinations of emotions. Some come from brutalizing experiences, some from a birthday celebration; some are full of hate at what has been done to them, others brimming with joy over the incredible beauties of the day. When the congregation is led in praying Psalm 56, the prayer seethes with experiences of brutality and hate. Hate is the most remote thing from my life right now, but within moments I am praying the experience of hate, in tune with others who may be experiencing it . . . . I enter into common cause with persons who are desperately facing enemies . . . . The psalms help take us to the place where we pray on behalf of others. [1]

Praying the Psalms together in the congregation conditions us to pray them much better when we are alone. They not only rescue us from repetition and move us out of our self-absorbed prayers, but they connect us with the feelings of others as well. And they empower us to break out of ourselves.

In 2009, my physicians detected cancer in my right lung. When I heard my doctor tell me I had cancer—a potentially fatal cancer—I had one of those out of body experiences. This is me the doctor is talking about, not someone else. I've gone through these experiences with so many other people and seen the stages of shock and disbelief and confusion and resolve to fight the cancer. I resolved quickly to fight this cancer that already was in advanced stages. We would have to act quickly. Surgery and chemotherapy and radiation would begin soon. I received letters and cards from hundreds of people, assuring that they were praying for us. Whether God chooses to heal me or not, the strength and courage flowing from the prayers of others is enormous.

What would happen? Would I be healed? Would I die within a year? I did not know. What I did know, however, is that whether God chooses to heal me or not, the strength and courage flowing from the prayers of others kept me taking the next step, waking up and taking on the next day of chemo or radiation or surgery.

Sometimes I find myself unable to pray. Some people call this "prayer block." I want assurance of God's presence, of his watchful care. At times I wonder, "Where is God?" Sometimes I cannot sense his presence. Some nights I toss in moods of morose darkness. There is a dark corner in our bedroom, to the right of the foot of our bed. Some nights I imagine God, if he is near at all, to be hiding himself in that corner. But I want him to come out. Sometimes I pray with Moses, "Lord, show me your glory." I am not sure what I am asking. I have often needed assurance, but no response came from that shadowy corner.

I have felt self-absorbed and guilty asking that I be singled out for healing. But wouldn't it be faithless not to ask for healing? Sometimes my prayers lock up completely. And just when this happens, postings and notes from hundreds of people literally all over the globe uphold me, assuring Carolyn and me of their love and prayer. Soon I begin to feel reassured. And maybe in these dark moments it does not matter that I can't pray, because their prayers sustain me.

How can I describe the sense of hope and comfort and assurance that began to creep back into me? I saw God show me his glory in hundreds of ways that I wish I could adequately describe. Sometimes, even in the midst of my times of prayer lock and doubt, I can still sense God's presence, even his glory and power.

When I think about how powerful these prayers of others have been in my life, it leads me to question, How does one become a person of prayer on behalf of others?

I do not have the full answer to this question. It is clearly beyond me to know all the ways God works through the prayers of others. But this much I do know: reading through psalms, praying and singing psalms, can move us out of ourselves and into a rich variety of prayers—including prayers of petition for others. These prayers from the Psalms also move us into the heart of God, the God for others.

For example, praying Psalm 61 for others may go something like this:

O God hear my prayer for my children, James and Molly
    and my grandchildren, Rebecca and Jeffery.
You have given them a heritage of those who fear and love you.
Give them grace when they don't pay attention to you. You are
    so patient with us!
Would you show my co-worker, Stan, that you are a rock that
    is higher than him?
You are a strong tower in his life as he goes through cancer
    treatment. Shelter him under the shadow of your wings.
O God, let my family, my co-workers, my church, my neigh-
    bors—your creation, God, all of it—dwell in your tent.
I can't speak for all of them, Lord, but I want to dwell in your
    tent forever! May they also dwell in your tent forever, O
    God!

Each psalm begins as a cry or petition or praise or lament of the original writer, but as we read it, we begin to pray the psalm for ourselves. Then we break out of ourselves and begin to pray the psalm for others. The variety of topics keeps our prayers fresh, allowing us to speak what was once unspeakable, go to places that were once uncomfortable, break out of ourselves into God's incredibly huge and ever-expanding reality!

The following are a selection of psalms and themes to illustrate how praying them can help us break out of ourselves and pay attention to God's goodness. For example, sometimes the Psalms simply and bluntly offer God's people strength and peace. One example is Psalm 29:11:

The LORD gives strength to his people;
> the LORD blesses his people with peace.

Psalm 121 offers us God's watchfulness and protection, "both now and forevermore." Psalm 23 promises everything I need.

Psalm 19 assures us that God's word "makes wise the simple," brings "joy to the heart and light to the eyes." His word also supplies "warnings and rewards."

Psalm 136 reminds us over and over that God's love is "steadfast and endures forever"—twenty-six times in this one psalm.

Psalm 41 offers deliverance in trouble, and the comfort that God will sustain us on our sick bed.

Psalm 103 lists an array of benefits: God can forgive all your sins, heals your diseases, satisfies your desires with good things, brings justice for the oppressed, and his love extends as high as the heavens, promising a mighty separation from our sins as far as the east is from the west.

Centering on God, his steadfast love, his deliverance, and his benefits gets us out of ourselves and reminds us he rules the universe.

Another way to break out of ourselves is to pray psalms that help us examine our own anxiety and lay it before God. My friend Marvin Bryant prays Psalm 139:23-24 regularly, sometimes rewording the essential thought, sometimes using the exact wording:

Search me, O God, and know my heart;
> test me and know my anxious thoughts.
See if there is any offensive way in me, and lead me in the
> way everlasting.

We often zero in on sinful thoughts of the heart, but Psalm 139 is a prayer for God to test and know our "anxious thoughts." Even scientific studies have shown that anxiety does damage to people and relationships. Systems theory or medicine, however, can't reveal what's in the heart. Only God can do that.

When we ask God to search our hearts, much of what is revealed isn't pretty. Marvin said asking God to search his heart has helped him break free from himself. "I've been shocked and amazed to find so much mixed, impure motivation, negative feelings, sinful desires, and anxiety in my heart." Marvin said. "But the presence of those things in our hearts makes the prayer of Psalm 139:23-24 so relevant and needed."

As we've discussed in this chapter, breaking free from ourselves is the pathway to something bigger than ourselves. But this breaking free is not the goal, just a portal to something unimaginable when we are still focusing on ourselves. The Psalms will not only lead us out of ourselves and into the lives of others but into the heart of God. Remember the goal of talking back to God in the Psalms is to pursue, not prayer methods, but God himself.

The ultimate purpose of prayer is not to get God to do what we want, but for us to become what he wants. I've had this brief but powerful prayer taped to the bottom of my computer for years. I was afraid to pray it for a while, but eventually I started praying it regularly. And it's never meant more to me than it does right now.

Lord, I am willing—
To receive what you give

To lack what you withhold
To relinquish what you take
To suffer what you inflict
To be what you desire

Reflection

1. What do you think about the connection between the Lord's Prayer and the Psalms?

2. Describe any "prayer formulas" you currently use, such as "Help. Wow. Thank you."

3. How do these words find expression in the Lord's Prayer?

4. What are some ways you need the Psalms to help you break out of yourself?

Action

1. Read or say aloud the Lord's Prayer from Matthew 6:9-13.

2. Read or say aloud the Lord's Prayer a second time. This time notice the personal but not individual language.

3. Read the Lord's Prayer aloud a third time. Notice the cosmic language.

4. Read Psalm 136 together in a group. Have one person read the different lines and the group recite the refrain again and again: *His love endures forever.*

5. Begin compiling your own list of discoveries about the purposes of prayer that you are learning from the rich variety and depth of the Psalms.

Chapter 8

FINDING STRENGTH IN OUR WEAKNESS

*"The work of prayer is to bring these two realities
together—the boldness of the Psalms and the extremity of our
experience—to let them interact, play with each other,
tease each other, and illuminate each other."*[1]

—Walter Brueggemann

Soon after I was diagnosed with lung cancer, I tossed through some long nights with dark shadows and my faith seemed terribly weak. Several mornings in a row, my first waking thought was, *I have death in my body.*

I must say that I did not take every thought captive, as Paul says, but that thought got away from me like a runaway stallion. *I have death in my body*, and *I may actually die from this.*

So one of those dark mornings I ventured to confess this to Carolyn.

"I have death in my body," I said.

"Of course you do," she replied. "So do I. So does everyone. But you also have life in your body. And we are going to celebrate life."

What an amazing word of light and hope my wife spoke to me that morning. She did take every thought—and word of mine—captive! She spoke truth and life to me in a dark, doubt-filled moment.

These intense emotions and the decision to live life tattooed the next discovery on our minds: *Praying the Psalms gives us strength in the midst of our weaknesses.*

Around this time, an email came from Jim McGuiggan, my dear friend in Ireland. He has walked through years watching his wife Ethyl suffer enormously, and he cared for her, happily waiting on her hand and foot. He knows something—well, much—about suffering. In his email, Jim said, "I'm glad that you look out your window and note that the sun's still shining, children are still laughing." Then he quoted from a poem by G. K. Chesterton. Interesting and lengthy, but these two lines jumped out at me.

There is one sin: to call a green leaf grey,
Whereat the sun in heaven shuddereth.

Carolyn said, "We are choosing to live 'in the green leaf.'" We will celebrate the good things in life—whatever life we have—and not miss the best of living each day because we are preoccupied with the possibility of dying.

This was a pivotal moment in processing my circumstances. This poem taught us to look for God's glory in this ordinary life—to see that God was showing his glory all along, his strength in our weakness.

Since those dark mornings, I've prayed Psalm 3—a lot.

Oh Lord, how many are my foes!
> How many rise up against me!
Many are saying of me,
> "God will not deliver him."
But you are a shield around me, O Lord.
> you bestow glory on me and you lift up my head.
In those dark corner moments I prayed, "Show me your
> glory. Take my eyes off the grey leaf. Give me eyes to see
> and celebrate the green."

Then I prayed Psalm 13:1-2,

How long, Oh Lord? Will you forget me forever?
> How long will you hide your face from me?
How long must I wrestle with my thoughts and every day
> have sorrow in my heart?

From my heart and mouth the words came out like this: "Come out of your dark corner and show me your glory! Somehow assure me of your presence."

I am not sure what I was asking for. Did I want God to glow in the dark corner? Did I want him to speak words aloud to me? Did I want him to sweep me up into the third heaven?

But gradually God began giving us eyes to see the glory he had been showing all along. There was plenty of "green leaf" right before me. But I had been distracted by the grey. Someone else sent me another poem that continued to open my eyes, and it goes like this:

A man cried out in despair,
"Touch me God, and let me know you are here."

Whereupon, God reached down and touched the man.
But, the man brushed the butterfly away . . . and walked on.[2]

In this simple nursery rhyme, I found a great reminder that God is always around us in the small and simple things we take for granted—not just in those rare sensational moments. Over and over the Psalms remind us to pay attention to God's glory in what may seem like ordinary circumstance in life, even in our dark moments, even in our weakness.

My Irish friend concluded, "Don't miss out on a blessing because it isn't packaged the way that you expect." Then one day later, three of our grandkids came by just to visit a few hours and play a game of cards. They opened my eyes to a wonderfully green leaf—a glimpse of glory.

Just outside our kitchen window, a family of bright red cardinals nested. Over many days we watched the little males steadily turn from grey to red. More glory!

Most days we could look out the bedroom glass doors and watch a majestic white tail buck drinking from our watering trough in the backyard; and sometimes a doe and twin fawns appeared. Glory grew!

Carolyn gave names to the green lizards that dart about on the porch railings. She pointed to God's glory in a Spanish Olive tree in the front yard bearing lush white blossoms from early spring till late fall. Glory upon glory.

Thunderheads billowed in the West Texas sky, snowy white against the azure blue, then sunset brought a slowly changing color from blue to bold orange flames. Squirrels chattered on oaks limbs. Brilliantly colored painted buntings, blue jays, robins, and cardinals joined the white doves that swarmed the backyard bird feeders. Green leaf upon green leaf—things I'd never fully appreciated though they'd been around me all along. But now I had to slow down and pay attention to God's glory.

One night we heard a soft noise at the front door and when we peeked out, there was a huge porcupine making his retreat down the steps. On early walks we felt the sweetness of the morning breeze and admired the bright yellow Esparanza, watched a humming bird dance above a blossom. I sat on the deck in the morning, feeling Carolyn's warm smile and kiss—a sweet glimpse of God's glory.

In the language of Henry Blackaby, we need to watch for where God is at work and go there. I was out of touch with reality—God is at the center of all reality, and I was only in touch with his absence. I wanted God to show up in my world, when I needed to show up in his! I thought he would pamper me by glowing in the dark for me. I'm not saying those things never happen, but this is a distorted view of God. God was with me all along. He had already shown up—it was me who needed to show up before God.

The Psalms are flooded with reminders to watch for God's presence and care through nature's wonders and ordinary events. In our growing relationship with God, these Psalms supply a way of praying that deepens our relationship and can become as natural as breathing. And in our weakness, these Psalms supply great strength.

Psalm 23 is one we return to time after time, and because it is so popularly quoted, we might tend to overlook the richness of this incredible psalm. Popular imagination pictures David writing Psalm 23, a shepherd boy sitting on a hillside with his sheep grazing quietly in the background as words of poetry spilled from his pen.

My own imagination resonates with John Killinger, who sees David, now the seasoned king, with his armies camped somewhere the night before a major battle. He sits by the campfire, taking in the evening sounds, the murmurs and clinking swords of his restless men. From across the valley, where enemy campfires flicker, he hears drunken laughter. Dawn will fill the valley with the thunder of hooves, the ring of steel—and the screams of the dying. Maybe David's own death cry!

But tonight, as he muses about life and death, he recalls God's faithfulness. His heart is full of warm memories of life in the pasture, when the very lives of his sheep depended upon his watchful presence. How secure he had felt as one of God's sheep, with the Lord as his shepherd!

How far David had come since those days as a shepherd boy! How different was commanding soldiers from watching sheep! Yet one thing hadn't changed: the God who watched over a shepherd still watched over a king! Even here in the "shadows of death."[3]

This scene is only one of many interpretations of the background and writing of Psalm 23. But it is one of the most likely scenarios. Though we don't really know when or where this psalm was composed, some scholars think it was after David became king.

While the background is unclear, Psalm 23 is very clear about these two things:

God is all we need.
God is always with us.

No matter what life brings me today, God is all I need and always with me. Psalm 23 certainly is assuring me of these two facts today. In battling cancer, I've faced some frightening and unpleasant prospects, and I can only imagine what today would be like without a shepherd.

If someone were to convince me that there is no loving shepherd, it seems to me that life's Un-Psalm would sound something like this:

Not: *The Lord is my shepherd, I shall not want:*
But: I am a sheep without a shepherd. I do not know who to follow—and I am utterly in want.

Not: *He makes me lie down in green pastures. He leads me besides still waters*
But: I am empty. Nothing satisfies. Nothing refreshes me. I find no real fulfillment. No lasting security. No real rest.

He restores my soul
I feel like a lost soul—totally, irretrievably depleted.

Even when I walk through the valley of the shadow of death, I will fear no evil, for you are with me
I don't believe anyone walks with me in the darkest valley! And contemplation of my own mortality holds me "all my life-time in bondage under fear of death"—for in that final hour I will be profoundly alone!

Your rod and your staff they comfort me
I feel misguided and I find no authentic comfort in anything. None.

You prepare a table before me in the presence of my enemies
I feel unwelcome in my world, always hungry for something—

and totally overwhelmed by a thousand threatening forces.
You anoint my head with oil. My cup runs over.
My blistered head aches, with no oil of relief. My joy cup is dry
all the way to the bottom. Bone dry.
Surely goodness and mercy will follow me all the days of my life
I have given up hoping for any real quality to my life.
In fact, genuine goodness and mercy have eluded me
all of my days—and I don't really expect things to change
And I will dwell in the house of the Lord forever.
Oh, how I ache to belong somewhere.
But don't really feel at home anywhere
And I think I will feel lonely and homeless forever.[4]

I feel great peace in seeing the reverse of Psalm 23—the Un-Psalm 23. When I think about what it would be like to live without God, I appreciate all the more his presence in my life. Psalm 23 is one of the greatest psalms of all that points to God who supplies our every need and gives us strength in times of weakness.

How radically counter-cultural! God supplies all we need. We twenty-first century North Americans are conditioned to be incomplete and unfulfilled without our stuff, space, safety, and security. But the psalmist subverts this dominant world view. God is the *only necessity of life*—because he provides all other necessities.

At the heart of Psalm 23 is the phrase, "for you are with me." God's almighty and loving presence is profoundly with us, even in our dark valleys! Of course there are other dark valleys besides death. In fact, the word "death" is not in the original text of Psalm 23. Your dark valley is wherever Psalm 23 may be catching up with you today.

The good news here is not that "having religion takes away the dark valleys." The real good news is that Yahweh walks through the dark valleys with us! His presence overcomes our fear of the darkness.

John Killinger once heard a man in London say, "You know, sometimes I miss those nights we spent in the Underground during the war, with firebombs falling on the city. Things mattered then in a way they haven't seemed to matter since. You knew God was around. You knew what life was about."

Oh yes! Dark valleys can even be the best times for thinking about God—not just when things run smoothly. Let something big happen and everything flips into a new dimension. Suddenly God becomes very real and important, front and center in the picture.

If David did write Psalm 23 by the light of a military campfire the night before a battle, the phrase, "in the presence of my enemies" would bring things into sharp focus. So right there in the midst of it all, David sees God "setting a table" for him—the banquet is God! The presence of David's enemies brought God into sharper focus.

Can you imagine God spreading a table for you? He spreads his table in some surprising places, and we can experience this if we have eyes to see. A powerful example of this truth occurred in the life of Victor Frankl during World War II. Frankl was put in a Nazi concentration camp with fellow Jews. They worked long days on meager, thin soup—it could not even be called eating or nourishment.

Early one winter morning Frankl and his fellow prisoners were marched off for another long day of hard labor. Many were sick. Most had lost loved ones to death in the camp. Everything they owned had been taken away from them. That day they had staggered back to the dormitories at dusk. As they sprawled on the narrow bunks, exhausted, a friend burst through the door, shouting for them to come outside. They dragged themselves out the door to be greeted by an extravagant sunset! The grey metallic clouds had broken open, and a riot of color splashed across the sky and reflected in the pools of water around the concrete courtyard. That bedraggled, broken little group of men stood there in awe, staring at the miracle of the sunset. And their hearts were lifted by that simple gift.

The sunset was to them a table spread in the presence of their enemies. The bursting colors in the sky reminded them of God's loving sovereign presence in a world where hate and wrong seemed to prevail.[5]

If we pay attention, we may still find God spreading surprise banquet tables in the midst of our darkest times. He is spreading mine while I write these lines.

If—as Killinger and I imagine—David composed Psalm 23 as a warrior king staring down real-life enemies, he knew the odds. Yes, God had kept him alive so far. But tomorrow might well be his time to take a lethal arrow or be thrust through by a sword. Yet, though surely he desired to live, he was nonetheless ready to die. "Surely goodness will pursue me," he said, "and I shall dwell . . . ."

Don't miss the second affirmation here: The first affirmation is that God will pursue, chase down, and grab hold of me with his righteousness. And the second is that unshakeable resolve—I will dwell!

The house of the Lord is anywhere God is, says Leroy Garrett. He explains that when we say with David, "I will dwell in the house of the Lord forever," we are saying nothing about a temple, heaven, or the church house. "The house of the Lord is any place where God is. So to 'dwell in the house of the Lord' is to be with God wherever we are or whatever befalls us."[6]

The overwhelming implication of being in the presence of God is that he gives us great strength in our weakness. That statement Carolyn and I came up with together encourages us daily: "We will celebrate the good things in life—whatever life we have—and not miss the best of living each day because we are preoccupied with the possibility of dying."

Even when we are too weak to see it ourselves, the Psalms remind us of God's strength available to us. They remind us that we can talk back to God—even when we feel as if death is in our bodies. We can shout in anger or whisper a desperate plea. We might even be so weak and numb that words or whispers fail us. In those moments when all hope seems to be drained out of life, God shows us his glory. The Psalms tell how God has done this for his people. And that's what God has done for me over and over—he's shown me his glory, his strength in my weakness, and he shines through in the big things and the small. All around us everyday, God supplies great strength in our weakness.

Reflection

1. Describe a time when the Psalms supplied strength to you in a time of great weakness.

2. Reflect on this quote by Walter Brueggemann: *"The work of prayer is to bring these two realities together—the boldness of the Psalms and the extremity of our experience—to let them interact, play with each other, tease each other, and illuminate each other."*

3. What are some of the realities the psalmists were living with and which are reflected in the Psalms?

4. What realities do you live with that you present before God in prayer? What realities do you not present before God in prayer?

Action

1. Go back to Un-Psalm 23 and read through it, but this time add your own experiences.

2. Write your own Un-Psalm 23. When you write, don't worry about presenting it to someone else, or about grammar, spelling, and eloquence.

PART IV

MINISTRY

Chapter 9

PRAYING WITH JESUS

May the words of my mouth and the meditation of my heart
be pleasing in your sight, O Lord, my Rock and my Redeemer.
—Psalm 19:14

Jesus prayed the Psalms in important moments in his ministry, but I didn't know this early in my life and ministry. The sooner we realize how valuable the Psalms have been in the spiritual lives of the ancients, including Jesus, the more we will want to join them. *The goal of this chapter is to show how Jesus interacted with the Psalms and used them in his ministry.*

Did Jesus know the Psalms? Absolutely. Many phrases from the Psalms fall from the lips of Jesus at pivotal moments. He was so full of the Psalms that they naturally spilled out. Speaking phrases from the Psalms seemed for him almost as natural as inhaling and exhaling. Gospel writers quote the Psalms two dozen times or more. Half of those are attributed to Jesus. One such occasion that comes to my mind is that dark day when Jesus was suspended by spikes from the cross, hovering between life and death. The words Jesus spoke on the cross, "Eloi, Eloi, Lama sabachthani?" or "My God, my God, why have you forsaken me?" (Matthew 27:46), come directly from Psalm 22. Many words of the Psalms were etched on Jesus' heart. Even in deepest suffering, he drew upon them to express what he was going through. These experiences connected with God's people who asked the same question in Psalm 22.

Why did Jesus cry out to God in this way? First, this was not an uncommon way for Jews to express their inner turmoil and grief. Second, when Jews heard this, they could have connected this messiah with the one whom the prophets spoke of and whom the Psalms call "Lord." No messiah of theirs would be ignorant of these words, the ancient expressions of the Jewish faith. The connections Jesus makes to the Psalms are vital for the Jews to understand him as the messiah—the anointed savior—of God.

But there is a secret to find in the Psalms, says Bonhoeffer, when we listen closely to the more difficult ones. "A psalm that we cannot utter as a prayer, that makes us falter and horrifies us, is a hint to us that here Someone else is praying, not we; that the One who is here protesting his innocence, who is invoking God's judgment, who has come to such infinite depths of suffering, is none other than Jesus Christ himself."[1]

Yes, the voice of the suffering Christ can be found in the Psalms. Jesus prayed the Psalms. Even on the cross. Scot McKnight says that the book of Psalms was "the prayer book Jesus used." Ever wonder what Jesus prayed in those early morning times on the mountain? We don't know exactly what he prayed on the mountain, but we do know the Psalms were an important part of Jesus' prayer life. "Jesus was a master of the Psalms," McKnight says. "Wherever he heard them, in the synagogue and at the temple, he took them to heart, for the Psalms spilled constantly from his lips. Because of this, anyone who follows Jesus into the Church to pray will quickly learn that praying with Jesus means using the Psalms: His entire life was bathed with psalms."[2]

McKnight points out that the Beatitudes pronounce blessings that come from the Psalms. "Blessed are the meek" was first found in Psalm 37. When opponents pressed Jesus, Mark shows Jesus quoting from Psalm 118, "The stone that the builders rejected has become the cornerstone." The fact that Jesus read, prayed, sang, and memorized the Psalms, directs us to also pursue the Father's heart through these ancient words.

But how did Jesus come to learn and memorize Psalms and voice them in his ministry? He participated in the life of the synagogue, where Psalms were read and heard weekly, says McKnight. "The book of Psalms was the first teacher and mentor in prayer for all of Judaism. So, Jesus followed the Jewish custom of learning the psalms, and he learned to make the psalms his own prayers."[3]

Bingo! McKnight hits directly on the goal in talking back to God: making these psalms our own prayers in our pursuit of God. So, believers who long for a deeper walk with God are following a path Jesus walked, saying and singing Psalms Jesus said and sung. Believers through the ages longing for this deeper walk, sooner or later, turn to the Psalms.

My friend Lee Patmore says he was blown away when someone pointed out to him that Jesus immersed himself in the Psalms. He had read them, memorized them, and prayed them. Then he realized that

Jesus' words of agony on the cross were not some carefully rehearsed quotes that the divine Son said merely to fulfill ancient prophecies. They were words of prayer that the Son of God had embraced and made his own that came from the Psalms. Jesus grew up memorizing and meditating on the Psalms. Armed with this new insight, Lee began his own journey through the Psalms. He says one fact drives his new practice of memorizing and meditating on the Psalms: Jesus did it, too.

For the ancient Hebrews, committing psalms to memory would have been different from the way we usually memorize Scripture. It was simply part of their regular life in the Scriptures. The ancient Hebrews would chant, sing, and speak psalms. The tunes were different from ours, the language was different, the meter and rhymes different from our English poetry and the tunes we often use. Over and over they would rehearse the story of God's mighty acts, lament oppression by occupying powers, praise God for rescuing them from the pit or the trap of sin or an enemy's attack.

Jesus would have read and heard these psalms in the synagogue each week. We can imagine that the tunes used to sing them would have been often on his heart. And he would have sung those together with others at various times. One of the most incredible exchanges that shows Jesus' knowledge and interaction with the Psalms comes in Matthew's Gospel. Matthew 21 describes the triumphal entry of Jesus.

When the religious leaders saw Jesus riding a donkey, saw people laying down palm branches, even clothing for the donkey to walk upon, they were angry. Why? Because he was being treated as a king—and

accepting the treatment! What made it worse was that children and
adults were singing psalms to Jesus. They sang from Psalm 118:26,

"Hosanna to the Son of David!"
"Blessed is he who comes in the name of the Lord!"
"Hosanna in the highest!"

What were they saying? Hosanna is an expression that means,
"Save!" The lines were familiar from the Psalms, but they applied them
to Jesus.

When Jesus entered the city and went into the Temple courts, he
overturned the tables of those selling animals for sacrifice. Jesus ac-
cused them of being thugs who had turned God's house into a den of
robbers.

The blind and the lame came to him at the Temple, and he healed
them. But when the chief priests and the teachers of the law saw the
wonderful things he did and the children shouting in the temple area,
"Hosanna to the Son of David," they were angry.

"Do you hear what these children are saying?" they asked him.
"Yes," replied Jesus, "have you never read,
"'From the lips of children and infants
you have ordained praise'?"

Here Jesus quotes from Psalm 8:2, returning indignant response for
indignant question, further angering them.

Later Jesus comes back to Psalm 118 when he tells the parable
of the tenants. The parable is about the religious leaders rejecting
the Messiah, and the line about a rock getting tossed aside but later

becoming the chief corner foundation stone of the new house of the Lord comes from Psalm 118:22-23:

> The stone the builders rejected
>> has become the capstone;
> the LORD has done this,
>> and it is marvelous in our eyes.

The rest of Psalm 118:24-29 describes a festal procession—not unlike the one that just took place—with children singing about the salvation of the Lord!

> This is the day the LORD has made;
>> let us rejoice and be glad in it.
> O LORD, save us;
>> O LORD, grant us success.
> Blessed is he who comes in the name of the LORD.
>> From the house of the LORD we bless you.
> The LORD is God,
>> and he has made his light shine upon us.
> With boughs in hand, join in the festal procession
>> up to the horns of the altar.
> You are my God, and I will give you thanks;
>> you are my God, and I will exalt you.
> Give thanks to the LORD, for he is good;
>> his love endures forever.

So, what are we to make of Jesus' interaction with the Psalms?

First, in moments of great importance, Jesus connects with the Psalms. The Gospel writers know how important this is to convey to readers who, like Jesus, were nurtured by Psalms in the synagogue and knew their gravitas.

Second, Jesus quotes the Psalms to point out bad religious thinking and to oppose evil. When Jesus enters the time of his betrayal, he quotes a psalm of David. David faced bitter opposition and betrayal and Psalm 41 is one way he processed the emotions and thoughts that come from being stabbed in the back by family and friends. So by quoting Psalm 41, Jesus also identifies with those who have been opposed by evil power brokers through history.

Third, he quotes Psalms to show unity with the Jewish experience—even though he opposes religious leaders gone bad, he doesn't oppose the longstanding faith of Israel. Jesus doesn't reject Jewish history and Scripture but engages it often to show his connection to the trajectory of God's story. As the Gospel of John records in John 13:18, Jesus is speaking to his disciples when he quotes a psalm of David. Like David, Jesus is greatly troubled about being betrayed by close loved ones. From Psalm 41:9, Jesus says, "He who shares my bread has lifted up his heel against me."

Fourth, Jesus identifies with the words of the Psalm as he goes through the grief of leaving his closest friends, the disciples. In Jesus' final discourses—found in the Gospel of John—he gives final instructions to his disciples. The instruction is full of love and the promise of the Holy Spirit to guide them. But Jesus quotes a vengeance Psalm of David! In John 15:25, Jesus says, "But this is to fulfill what is written in their Law: 'They hated me without reason.'" This appears to be a direct quote from Psalm 35:19. And Psalm 35 is filled with words of vengeance toward those who hate without cause:

> Contend, O LORD, with those who contend with me;
> > fight against those who fight against me.
> Take up shield and buckler;
> > arise and come to my aid.
> Brandish spear and javelin
> > against those who pursue me.
> > Say to my soul,
> > "I am your salvation."
> May those who seek my life
> > be disgraced and put to shame;
> > may those who plot my ruin
> > be turned back in dismay. (Psalm 35:1-4)

The Psalms come back to God's rule. Over and over again the psalmists put their trust in God. They lay down their burdens before Almighty God. They commit everything—body and soul—to God.

Throughout his life, Jesus points to God's rule, his kingdom. Even on the cross, Jesus commits his body and soul to the Father. The words Jesus utters on the cross are similar to a line in Psalm 31:5, recorded in Luke 23:46, "Father, into your hands I commit my spirit."

From first to last, the Psalms were part of Jesus life. They must have permeated his childhood. We have seen evidence that Psalms were certainly important to his ministry. See the chart below that shows how Jesus interacted with the Psalms in the Gospels.

Jesus and Psalms		
Four to show the religious leaders their mistaken position	Matthew 21:16 Matthew 21:42, Mark 12:10-11, Luke 20:17 Matthew 22:44, Mark 12:36, Luke 20:42-43 John 10:34	Psalm 8:2 Psalm 118:22-23 Psalm 110:1 Psalm 82:6
Four to denounce those that worked evil & misunderstood Jesus' teaching	Matthew 7:23 Matthew 13:35 Matthew 25:41 Luke 13:27	Psalm 6:8 Psalm 78:2 Psalm 6:8 Psalm 6:8
Two in dialogue with disciples in last 24 hours	John 13:18 John 15:25	Psalm 41:9 Psalm 35:19, 69:4
Two from the cross	Matthew 24:46, Mark 15:34 Luke 23:46	Psalm 22:1 Psalm 31:5
One in temptation in wilderness (Satan quotes)	Matthew 4:6, Luke 4:10-11	Psalm 91:11-12

Chart Source: http://www.thebibletrue.info/

Reflection

1. Use the chart in this chapter to read and reflect on the Psalms quoted in the Gospels by Jesus.

2. How do some of the events described in the Psalms also describe what Jesus was experiencing with his opponents and disciples?

Action

1. From the chart, choose one of the Psalms Jesus quotes in the Gospels.

2. Memorize this portion of the Psalm Jesus quotes.

3. Dig deeper into the original context of the Psalm you choose.

4. Dig deeper into the context of the Gospel story where Jesus quotes the Psalm.

Chapter 10

MINISTERING LIKE JESUS

The Psalms are "shockingly alien; creatures of unrestrained
emotion, wallowing in self-pity, sobbing, cursing, screaming
in exultation . . . . we shall find in the Psalms expressions of a
cruelty more vindictive and a self-righteousness more com-
plete than anything in the [Greek] classics. If we ignore such
passages and read only a few selected favourite Psalms, we
miss the point. For the point is precisely this: that these same
fanatic and homicidal Hebrews, and not the more enlight-
ened peoples, again and again—for brief moments—reach a
Christian level of spirituality. It is not that they are better or
worse than the Pagans, but they are both better and worse."
—C. S. Lewis, Christian Reflections[1]

Bringing what we're discovering together, take a moment to remember these benefits of praying the Psalms. Reading and then
praying the Psalms deepens your prayer life. Through the Psalms

we access the power of heaven, and this is vital to discipleship and leadership. Every disciple needs courage in the jaws of suffering and temptation, but leaders also need to access the power of God in ministry.

So the Psalms become effective tools for ministry. They give us mentoring and equipping skills. I've used the Psalms in mentoring for many years, and these ministry tools and equipping skills become leaven—a spreading agent—in local churches.

New Testament writers certainly lived in the Psalms and seemed to keep them always before the community of believers. They quote texts from the Old Testament more than three hundred times. Nearly one hundred of those quotes are fragments of the Psalms. The Gospel writers, Paul, the Hebrew author, and Peter all quote the Psalms.

Paul quotes Psalms more than any other New Testament writer. Romans alone has more quotes of the Psalms than are attributed to Jesus in the Gospels. In his letters, Paul quotes the Psalms twenty-four times. Three times in Acts, Luke records Paul quoting from the Psalms.

What is it about the Psalms that resonates with New Testament writers, the Jewish people, and the disciples of Jesus? *The goal of this chapter is to discover how Psalms can help us minister like Jesus.* Psalms were woven into the life and ministry of Jesus and his followers. So also psalms can be woven into our lives and ministries.

Paul is one of the first great examples of how a follower of Christ lived in the words of the Psalms. In Romans 3, Paul quotes from Psalms seven times. In Romans, Paul continues a great and enduring theme from the Psalms: the justice and compassion of God meets the sin and sorrow of humanity. As Psalm 85:10 says,

Love and faithfulness meet together;
righteousness and peace kiss each other.
Faithfulness springs forth from the earth, and righteousness
looks down from heaven.

Paul points to God who is loving yet will not overlook sin—the psalmists did this as well. Romans 3:10 is a frequently quoted line from Paul—"There is no one righteous, not even one"—which was part of a larger quote from Psalm 14:1-3 and Psalm 53:1-3. And he quotes Psalm 117:1 to emphasize that God's grace has come, not to Jews alone, but to all nations (Romans 15:7-11).

In the same way that Paul wrote to remind the churches of God's gracious story and how all have been invited into that adventure, so the Psalms include many such reminders. Psalm 78 and Psalm 107, for example, review the early history of God's people. Just as Paul reminds Jews and Gentiles alike that they have all sinned, so these two Psalms remind God's people that sin and rebellion have scarred and marred the image of God in them. But the reminder of God's justice comes with a redeeming recognition of his mercy as well.

How can Psalm 78 and Psalm 107 become tools for ministry? Consider what Paul did and what we can do with these Psalms. Paul took a church situation—a ministry context—and used the Psalms as tools to communicate a message. Jesus did this as well. The Psalms are not one dimensional—they address the enduring themes of God's story.

The Psalms were like glue holding together some of the teaching of the early church. One example of this use of the Psalms is how New Testament writers quoted the same Psalms. For example, John and Paul both quote different parts of Psalm 69 in their apostolic teaching (John 2:17; Romans 15:3). Psalm 69 seems to be one that became part of the fabric of the early church, and learning this psalm is valuable because of its significance to our Christian faith. They each quote different lines from Psalm 69 and draw different meanings from it—and that's the point. We bring our lives, our experiences, to the Psalms and they speak to our situations, point us to God's purposes in the world. Jesus did this, the apostles continued to do this, and we can, too.

We can take the same Psalm 69 and bring our own experiences to these ancient words and in many ways connect with ancient Israel, the early church, and, twenty-one centuries later, Christians today. For example, authors Peter Greer and Phil Smith have written an excellent book about helping the poor through business opportunities. They draw the title—*The Poor Will Be Glad*[2]—from Psalm 69:32-33:

> The poor will see and be glad—you who seek God, may your
> hearts live!
> The Lord hears the needy and does not despise his captive
> people.

Each of us can bring our own experiences to the Psalms and connect with the ministry of Jesus, the Apostles, and Christians through the ages. To understand the kind of currency the Psalms had in the life of the Jews and early Christians, remember the impact of Psalm 23 on us today. In a similar way that Psalm 23 is famous and often quoted, so also other psalms were famous and often quoted among Hebrews and early Christians.

Psalms were important to Jesus and the church. How then can they become important in our ministry? By reading, singing, praying, and memorizing them like Jesus and the early church did.

Of course, I do not profess to have such a psalm saturated subconsciousness like Jesus, Paul, or the writer of Hebrews. God has led me, however, into many crucial ministry moments when a psalm or psalmic phrase has popped out of my mouth almost before I knew what I was saying. I can't begin to remember all those moments, but some are unforgettable.

Earlier I told a story about a young Christian woman who came to talk with me, seemingly utterly depressed. The biggest problem she felt was not so much depression as being turned off by the constant, positive, upbeat, cheerleading style of the worship assemblies she experienced in her church. From everything she was being told at church, she thought God demanded a full-time positive mental attitude. She felt hopelessly shut out of "Christian normalcy."

Almost before I thought about it, we were reading Psalm 88 together—all dark throughout and ending with the words, "darkness is my only friend." This psalm gave her permission to have dark feelings. This became spiritual therapy to her as she discovered that permission and discovered that there are times when it is perfectly normal and healthy to pour out negative feelings of lament. Psalm 88 supplied in that setting what I had never thought of on my own—and it became a great tool for ministry.

Through this and other experiences pointing people to the Psalms, I have discovered that memorizing psalms can be an excellent beginner's tool for learning how to mentor others. Over many years of leading mentoring groups and individuals, I have developed a very simple plan that leads to spiritual growth.

In the early stages of a mentoring circle, I ask each person to tell his or her story—however long that takes; sometimes it takes as many as three or more meetings for everyone to tell their stories. I tell the group my story first to give the rest courage and a template. Sometimes this takes me as long as forty-five minutes because I want to shape out the basic facts first: Where were you born? What were your parents and siblings like and your relationship with them? Where did you go to school and what were your experiences like there? What important events happened in each stage of your life? If married, how did you meet your mate, and what is something significant to say about each of your children?

Then I lead them through the highs and low points of my Christian walk—how I came to Christ, my life's passion.

When the stories are over, I introduce them to the idea of praying and memorizing the Psalms. This takes little to no training in group dynamics. I encourage them to pick a psalm and pray it daily till our next meeting. With that psalm chosen, I give the group three steps. These are steps for living in the psalm and praying the psalm.

First, read the psalm aloud to get the overall feel and picture of the psalm.

Second, read the psalm aloud again, this time as your own prayer.

Third, read it aloud as your prayer on behalf of someone else that this psalm brings to mind.

I ask the group to be prepared to report at the next meeting what psalm they chose to pray and why, their understanding of the psalm, and what this experience meant to them, whether positive or negative. Eventually we add a memorizing piece. That is, we each pick a different psalm or significant section of a psalm to memorize each month. At our gatherings we each recite the chosen psalm and tell about times it has come to mind as an actual ministry tool. After each person recites a psalm, we pray for that person.

The storytelling and psalms function to give focus to the meetings of the mentoring circle. Everyone brings their own story and psalm, so the subjects keep changing, but the time together stays focused around this storytelling and psalm reciting framework. In this way, praying and memorizing the Psalms becomes in itself an excellent tool for ministry. Then I encourage the circle to start mentoring someone else.

If you are ready to try memorizing, a more detailed description follows in a later section of this book. If you want to start a group and use this simple but effective approach, first share your story, encourage others to share theirs, then start reading the Psalms. You don't have to know group dynamics—just tell stories, recite psalms, and pray.

What are we really doing in these groups? We're bringing our own experiences to the Psalms so that we can encounter God together. Ancient Jewish communities and early church assemblies encountered God in their gatherings as well, and part of those gatherings included reciting or singing from the Psalms. And like the ancient communities, these groups go out into the world on a mission to seek lost souls who are wandering apart from God. The Psalms lead us from our own experiences—good or bad—back to God.

In 1991, Debbie Dorman listened to a group of street kids at a youth retreat testify how God saved them from spiritual—and physical death—and incredibly, graciously gave their lives back. Soon after witnessing those life-changing moments in the lives of kids on the streets, Debbie read Psalm 124 as if for the first time, particularly the line, "The snare is broken and we have escaped!"

What happened next is a testimony to the life of the ancient Psalms still living in the fabric and ministry of a church Debbie is part of in Austin, Texas. Debbie joined a long line of people through the centuries who turned an experience of doubt and darkness into a new song of hope and light.

After Debbie read Psalm 124, a song came to her clearly and she wrote the lyrics and the tune at the piano that day for "Had It Not Been the Lord":

Had it not been the Lord who was on our side
  Had it not been the Lord who was on our side
The anger of the enemy would have swallowed us alive
  Had it not been the Lord who was on our side.

Had it not been the Lord who was on our side
  Had it not been the Lord who was on our side
The waters would have engulfed us, we would have surely
  died
  Had it not been the Lord who was on our side.

Blessed be the Lord who would not give us up
  Blessed be the Lord for His unfailing love
The snare is broken and we have escaped
  Our help is in the name of the Lord. Blessed be the
  Lord!

The song is amazingly simple yet it reaches into the depths of our fear of drowning in the overwhelming flood of life. The refrain, "Blessed be the Lord" is frequent in the Psalms and would have been on the lips of God's people often. God will not give us up! His love is unfailing! The psalmists recognized that the love of God has broken the snare of death and freed them from captivity. The waters have subsided, and safely on the other side of the troubled waters the worshipping community can say, "Our help is in the name of the Lord. Blessed be the Lord."

When Debbie read Psalm 124 the first time, she received the right combination of tune and words for the song. The song broke open the hearts of people in Hope Chapel when she sang it, and it continues to open people's hearts as they sing in many worshipping assemblies worldwide.

Making the Psalms a powerful part of ministry takes living in the words of the psalmists and not just reading, rote memory, or even singing alone. The Psalms must touch our lives and experiences.

To conclude this chapter, consider that Psalm 78 is much like our lives. We have ups and downs. Just as our own life stories are full of those swings, so is the story of God's people. Even a small slice of this psalm below, 78:35-40, shows the ebb and flow of life and God's response.

They remembered that God was their Rock,
   that God Most High was their Redeemer.
But then they would flatter him with their mouths,
   lying to him with their tongues;

their hearts were not loyal to him,
 they were not faithful to his covenant.
Yet he was merciful;
 he forgave their iniquities
 and did not destroy them.
Time after time he restrained his anger
 and did not stir up his full wrath.
He remembered that they were but flesh,
 a passing breeze that does not return.
How often they rebelled against him in the desert
 and grieved him in the wasteland!

Reflection

1. What was it the New Testament writers found in the Psalms?

2. How can we use psalms like these to minister to people who continually wonder whether God will be gracious to them in their mistakes?

3. How could memorizing be used as a tool for reminding people of God's great love and mercy?

Action

1. Pray Psalm 139:23-24 today.

2. Repeat the prayer daily for one week.

3. Write a journal entry about Psalm 139:23-24.

4. In your journal, write what God is showing you in response to the plea for God to search your heart?

PART V

WONDER

Chapter 11

BELONGING TO GOD

*Psalms are the spiritual "tribal" language of believers. This
language is of people who suffer, are desperate, and have
burned their bridges to any other solution except God, who
pause in mid-stampede and are undone by God's companion-
ship, and then search for words of gratitude.*
—Mark Abshier

*The Psalms remind us who we are, give us an identity and place to
belong in God's huge story.*

Dr. Scott Momaday, Regents' Professor of Humanities at the
University of Arizona, has known since childhood that he and his
family are Native Americans. His story illustrates how one family intentionally led a young boy to understand his identity. What young
Momaday found was a whole new identity that changed his life.

When Momaday was a child on the Kiowa reservation, his father
woke him up early one morning. "Son, it's time to go," he said. He took
the sleepy boy to the house of the "old one" and left him there all day.

After that day, Momaday would never be the same. The "old one" began to speak halting but spellbinding words to the boy, her tongue rich with the accents of the Kiowa people. She recited poems and chanted songs of the Kiowa. She told how the Kiowa had come from a hollow log in the Yellowstone River. She described how they grew as a tribe. She painted word pictures of buffalo hunts and fighting other tribes. Her eye narrowed as she seemed to relive hardships such as blizzards, the coming of the white man, the disappearance of the buffalo, starvation. He felt the humiliation and deprivation of the move south to Kansas and then to Oklahoma and finally to Fort Sill.

Riveted to his chair, young Momaday could have listened for days to these stories. When the sky grew red in the west, Momaday's father returned and said, "Son, it's time to go."

Momaday remembers that day as a day of transformation. "When I arrived at the house of the old one, I was a lad. When I left, I was a Kiowa," he said. Scott Momaday knows who he is because he knows his story. He is a Kiowa. For him, home isn't a place; it is joining the story of his people.

We believers in Jesus have roots and an identity, too. God's story tells us who we are, gives us a place to belong—not a physical place but a story or adventure to join. Of course, the story runs back far beyond a hollow log in the Yellowstone River. The story begins in the beginning with God himself.

God is our father, and we are his children. Psalm 95:7 says we are "the people of his pasture, the flock under his care." From Adam to Abraham, our story unfolds. Then on to Moses and to David, then forward. Our story continues through the manger, up Calvary, through Easter and Pentecost, and across the centuries until this very day.

Ours is the story of the people.

Of course, God knows each of us personally—even to the exact number of hairs on our heads, says Matthew 10:30. (After chemotherapy, this would be a quick count for my head!) He takes personal interest in us, even when we feel isolated from him and others. But God also knows we need much more than individual care. We do not flourish—don't even stay balanced—in isolation. So he keeps calling us together, drawing us out of our loneliness—at least some of it—and into circles of relationship. As the ancient Hebrew poet mused in Psalm 68:6, "God sets the lonely in families."

J. C. Bailey was the first evangelist God used to prick my father's heart. After hearing Bailey preach, Dad wrote that evening to his girlfriend, who would later become his wife and my mother:

Dear Mary,

Tonight I heard Bailey teach from the Bible. He talked about the church. He said the church is not a building. It is not an organization, nor a denomination. But that in the Bible, the church is just a circle of believers gathered around Jesus![1]

We live in what some have called a cut flower culture that places little value on heritage, has little patience or interest in history. Walter Brueggemann says the primal function of grandmas and grandpas is to help the grandchildren remember. "They are an active and intentional antidote," he says, "for the amnesia that grandchildren too readily practice."

Our branded consumerism invites all manner of people to buy and trade and consume and need, and keep all particularities

private and hidden. The delete button is an icon of amnesia . . .
just delete. Delete old memories. Delete old belongings. Delete
old embarrassing grandfatherly miracles and grandmotherly
narratives. Delete the past, and live in the present . . . world
without end, from strength to strength, from stratagem to
stratagem, from show to show, from game to game.[2]

Brueggemann says it was no different in ancient Israel. Would the
children get bored by the old stories? Would they get inpatient with
the recitation of the Exodus from Egypt, the wandering? Would they
be skeptical of the "mighty acts" that God performed in the desert and
on Mount Sinai? Indeed, they did get put out with the old ways, and
they craved contemporary and pagan cultures. In fact, Deuteronomy
is the repetition of the mighty acts of God and the law so that they
would not forget. Moses tells them not to forget how God led them out
of Egypt, through the desert, fed them, and brought them to their new
settlement. Do not get there and build nice houses and say to yourself,
"'My power and the strength of my hands have produced this wealth
for me.' But remember the LORD your God, for it is he who gives you
the ability to produce wealth, and so confirms his covenant, which he
swore to your forefathers, as it is today" (Deuteronomy 8:17-18).

Many of the Psalms are poetic recitations that help Israel remember. While some forgot their stories, and thus their identities, others
did remember. Hebrews told their children stories so they wouldn't
forget who they were.

Psalm 105, for example, reviews the story of the Exodus, which
reminds the Hebrews where they came from and who they are. While

Psalm 105 specifically tells the Exodus story in more narrative form, Psalm 107 helps make the story our own, a story for all people, "those he gathered from the lands, from east and west, from north and south." These psalms link us to our past in intimate and profound ways.

These psalms actually retrace the roots from which God's chosen people have come. When we read or memorize a psalm, we do more than digest information. We relive a story. This reminds us who we are and where we belong. The Christ-following community is an extension of the Hebrew people; the church is the new Israel.

Psalm 107 is a poetic recitation of the story that the Hebrews could connect to the Exodus or Exile in Babylon—times when God led them out and saved them with a mighty hand and an outstretched arm. We too can hear these words from Psalm 107:1-9 and remember how God has saved us in our desperate times:

Give thanks to the LORD, for he is good;
　　his love endures forever.
Let the redeemed of the LORD say this—
　　those he redeemed from the hand of the foe,
those he gathered from the lands,
　　from east and west, from north and south.
Some wandered in desert wastelands,
　　finding no way to a city where they could settle.
They were hungry and thirsty,
　　and their lives ebbed away.
Then they cried out to the LORD in their trouble,
　　and he delivered them from their distress.

He led them by a straight way
    to a city where they could settle.
Let them give thanks to the LORD for his unfailing love
    and his wonderful deeds for men,
for he satisfies the thirsty and fills the hungry with good things.

Not only do these psalms connect us with the ancient psalmists, but they also link us with first-century Christians as well. Since the Psalms were both hymnal and prayer book to the early church, when we pray them now in the twenty-first century, we pour out the very passions of the first Christian worshippers. We join hands and kneel in solidarity with them.

In fact, the Psalms fill our modern mouths with the very words whispered by terrified saints as they cowered in the Catacombs, or faced the terror of wild beasts unleashed on them, of swords wielded against them, and of the flames of Nero.

The Psalms also connect us with the triumphant vision of Reformation leaders. Many of the classic hymns we sing came from the book of Psalms. We raise our voices with the same lyrics that rose from their passionate hearts.

And Psalms link us to brothers and sisters around the globe who may at this very hour be under real persecution, losing jobs and homes and loved ones—even torture and death for the cause of Christ. Clinging to God through the lifeline of the Psalms, they have hope till their last breath. The words they pray in Afghanistan, Indonesia, India, Laos, the Middle East, China, and Africa may well be the very same words that tumble out of our mouths today. The Psalms.

Praying with the church worldwide using the Psalms helps us know who we are and where we belong. And when we know who we are, we know what we should do.

Imagine if we did not have the psalms that recite the story of God's mighty works in creation and among the Jewish people. What would happen if these stories did not exist? The problem is, these story psalms do exist, but we ignore them and consider them irrelevant to our lives. Walter Brueggemann warns us of such forgetfulness. He says, "Forget and you will have a world of no burning bush, no holy intrusion, no summons to freedom, no resolve from heaven to work newness on the earth."[3]

This generation does not seem to realize that much of its worldview—even its very identity—is shaped by all that has gone before. So sometimes we do not know who we are or where we belong. But the Psalms give us a place to belong. Praying the Psalms connects us with the long story of worshippers down through the centuries. Reading and reflecting on a particular psalm, digging into the context for it, connects us with the person who wrote it. We imagine the circumstances that prompted the psalm.

Memory and recitation and story are contained in the Psalms. Memory—reciting the story through the Psalms—leads to identity. What if we went back in time to help us see this more clearly? Imagine the Jews in 449 B.C.E., on a road near Jerusalem, just one year after the Hebrews returned to the Promised Land from their long exile in Babylon.

I'll be your guide. Let's go.

We're walking down the road outside of Jerusalem. Do you see the hills of the city? There's the road ahead of us leading into the city. People trudge up the trail toward you. But they appear to be celebrating.

"Excuse me," I ask the group, "but what's the happy occasion?"

One of the men beams and says, "We're returning from God's special meeting place."

"What did you do there?" I ask.

"You see this basket?" the man points to a large basket on his wife's head. "This is the basket that carried our firstfruits—the first grain from our field and first grapes from our vineyard."

The woman pulls the basket from her head and removes the cloth inside it, revealing an empty basket.

"So why are you pointing out the empty basket?" I ask.

"Oh, the basket is important. It doesn't just carry firstfruits. Our basket also carries a story. We call it a basket of memories," the man says.

"A basket of memories of what?"

"It helps us remember who God is," he said. "Some people go for what they get out of it, but my father says we go there to meet the One."

"Who is the One?" I ask.

"God himself. He is the real world. Father says we must do this to remember that God gave us everything we have, made us everything we are. Because, if we forget who God is, then we will forget who we are!"

In the grass and on boulders beside the road, the group sits down to rest, and the man tells a story.

"My father was a wandering Aramean, and he went down into Egypt with a few people and lived there and became a great nation, powerful and numerous. Of course, when we Hebrews say 'my father' we actually mean 'us'—our living selves and all of our ancestors. But the Egyptians mistreated us and made us suffer, putting us to hard labor. Then we cried out to the Lord, the God of our fathers (Deuteronomy 26:5-7).

Another traveler with a basket chimed in.

"Father says, 'God always hears the cries of suffering people. But he doesn't give a rat's whisker for wealth and power. Although God made Egypt wealthy, they did not acknowledge him. Instead, they used his wealth to build their own powerful empire—which made us slaves and intimidated their neighbors. Yet while Egypt's power expanded, our slave population exploded—till we outnumbered them, so the Pharaoh tried to kill all our baby boys.' But our mother hid her baby boy Moses at the river's edge—in a basket. God's irony: Pharaoh's own daughter raised Moses, the deliverer who broke Pharaoh's empire and brought us to this promised land."

A woman in the group could not contain her joy when she realized her people's connection to this story.

"Our deliverer came from the basket!" she says. "This morning we carried our deliverance story in our basket of memories. Mother says, 'If we forget our *deliverance story*, we may repeat the *empire story*: we start thinking we deserve our wealth, that we couldn't be happy without it, and then go to any lengths to maintain it. Empire thinking! And we'd end up abusing others the way Egypt abused us. The oppressed becoming the oppressors.'"

The first man with the basket reminded the group that their own King Solomon did that. He abused his power.

"Even though he was God's chosen king, Solomon forgot God. Then he got greedy and then fearful. He drafted huge armies. Built intimidating military bases—on the backs of slaves! He created a powerful and oppressive empire—a lot like Egypt! Then our kings after Solomon seemed stuck in the empire story," he says.

"But remember, Yahweh always hears the cries of suffering people—including our own suffering slaves! So eventually God smashed our empire and banished us to Babylon. Well, nowadays the countryside is abuzz over old Isaiah's radical poem. Here all these centuries later, we are out of Babylon and back in our land. But the cranky old poet fears our new King Hezekiah is headed back into empire thinking. Greed. Fear. Bad alliances. Yes, Isaiah's poem is a long confusing rant, but people get his point: 'You better get it right this time!' he warns, 'If you forget God again—and mistreat the poor and the aliens again—you will fail again, like you did back before the horrors of Babylon!'"

"Most people hate the old poet," the woman says. "But my parents agree with him. Mother says now that we are back in the land again we have a fresh shot at the 'peaceable kingdom' Isaiah talks about. But not if we forget."

"My father says, 'Our baskets of firstfruits will help us remember.'"

"What happened to all the firstfruits everyone took to the meeting place?" I ask.

"Ah, that's a great question—you see, the firstfruits we set before the altar this morning didn't just vanish into thin air. They went to real people—just as they did in our ancestors' day. Some went to our priests and our poor, of course. But, we gave some to the aliens among us as well. My father says, 'Don't miss this. We gave our best to strange-smelling, gibberish-talking, funny-dressed foreigners.'"

"We do this so we don't forget that we too were homeless aliens. Permanent trespassers. These trespassing aliens are part of our story. Part of us. Our kin. And you know what? God's heart also aches for these shunned foreigners we met today. The story is not just ours but theirs, too," the man says.

"So this afternoon we threw a party," the man continues. "We danced and sang with this swirling mix. Rich and poor. Hebrews and foreigners. We all felt remembered. No one going without. No one sitting alone. A brief glimpse of old Isaiah's peaceable kingdom—when Messiah comes."

"You have more than a basket of memories," I said. "You belong to a story of hope and a future!"[4]

This story is about the importance of identity. The basket of memories shaped the identity of the travelers in this story. For Scott Momaday, discovering his identify changed everything. Not having these Psalms would be like losing one's voice. My friend Marvin Bryant once lost his voice for such a long time that it truly affected his identity. And no wonder—imagine a preacher without a voice!

Marvin was forced into a five-month absence from preaching for surgery on his vocal chords. "What I love to do and feel called to do," Marvin recalled, "had been taken away from me. I felt weak, useless, vulnerable, whiny, uncertain about my future as a preacher and my calling. My sinful self-reliance was exposed. My tendency to try to gain validation through what I accomplish was exposed. I prayed that God would open my heart to feelings I had stuffed for years, help me get over the perfectionism I used to cover up my feelings. This ordeal certainly addressed all that."

Marvin said he really identified with Psalm 40 during this ordeal. "I felt like I was in the pit with the psalmist in Psalm 40!" he said. "I cried out to God and waited for him, sometimes patiently, sometimes not."

After months of prayer and gradual recovery, Marvin was allowed to preach again. God had raised him out of the pit of despair. The most wonderful part about it was the way God worked through his ordeal, he says, "to pierce my ears and write his word on my heart. In my younger years, I hid my feelings and longings for God behind academia. During my wilderness time, however, I realized God was doing to me what he did to this psalmist—he allowed adversity in my life to write the word on my heart."

So for Marvin, two particular truths of the word became clear: First, we really need to trust God. The psalmist learned this, too (Psalm 40:4-5). Second, God works through weakness. The second half of Psalm 40 reminds us that more struggle likely lies ahead. Sadly, but not surprisingly, even after having the word written on his heart, this psalmist still sinned and found himself in another mess. So he once again did what he had done before—cried out to the Lord.

Though weak and still struggling, the psalmist remembered the Lord. And crying out to the Lord brings us back to the story, to who we are and where we belong. This re-orientation to our identity as God's people helps us take the next step.

The following story illustrates what happens when a people loses their identity: they also lose their direction.

Timothy Dwight's story confirms that faithfully practicing the singing and learning of the Psalms can change the world. In 1795, Yale called upon Timothy Dwight to lead the college as president. In the first years as president of Yale, Dwight found students caught up in fervor for the French Revolution, rationalism, and science. They were far more interested in Voltaire and Paine than Moses and Christ. Their pursuit of philosophy and reason did not take them toward God but exalted human achievement. Yet they had no ethical foundation and the students degenerated into wild partying—this does not surprise us today, and even some college presidents today feel helpless to change this damaging, reckless way of life for college students. Against the odds, Timothy Dwight believed Yale students could change.

In those days, the president often also taught classes. Dwight taught theology classes, and he challenged his classes to debate the authenticity of the Bible as God's word. Most, if not all, the students took the negative argument, while Dwight argued for the affirmative. The Bible is God's true word to us and can change our lives.

Dwight also began preaching in the Yale Chapel week after week from 1795 to 1800, but only a few students attended, fewer yet became followers of Christ. During those years, Dwight was producing a new edition of the famous Isaac Watts hymnal (1719) entitled "The Psalms of David Imitated in the Language of the New Testament." In the course of bringing out that new edition, Dwight added some of his own work. There were evidently some Psalms omitted in the Watts book, and Dwight decided to include them.

Like Watts before him, Dwight was trying to "imitate the Psalms of David in the language of the New Testament." The song, "I Love Thy Kingdom, Lord" was inspired when Dwight was immersed in the Psalms. And Dwight sang this song often in the Yale Chapel, with those few students. In 1801-02, something happened that is nothing short of miraculous.

The Holy Spirit moved students to put their trust in God, and a third of the student body became Christians. Many signed up to go out on evangelistic missions, preach the gospel, and make disciples of Christ. Dwight's sharp teaching, determined leadership, and faithful attention to singing and hearing the Psalms led to renewed and faithful life among students. And these students, in turn, became leaders and carriers of the gospel all over the world.

This student movement sparked by Timothy Dwight—grandson of Jonathan Edwards, who preached in the "Great Awakening"—became part of what is now referred to as "The Second Great Awakening." Most Bible-believing churches in America today are heirs of that movement.

Praying the Psalms weaves us back into the family fabric, where we belong. When we pray the Psalms, we pray with ancient Hebrews, first-century Christians, and disciples across many movements such as the Reformation and the Great Awakening. For thirty centuries—three thousand years—people have been praying the Psalms. When we pray the Psalms, we share the identity of a long line of faithful people. When we pray the Psalms, Eugene Peterson points out that we are not by ourselves.

David danced these psalms before the Ark of the Covenant and the Hebrews in Solomon's Temple chanted them. Children running down the slope of Olivet waved palm branches and shouted these psalms, and Jesus in the upper room with his disciples sang them. The Corinthian Christians celebrated the Eucharist with these psalms and the apocalyptic 144,000 fill heaven with them.[5]

When we authentically read, pray, and sing these psalms today, we are worshipping with all believers of all times. And we know that we belong to them and to each other—and to God.

A story about the legendary Helen of Troy illustrates how important memory can be to shaping our identity. Helen of Troy was known as the face that launched a thousand ships. In one of the many wars over Helen of Troy, she was captured by barbarous and hostile peoples. They mistreated her, made her a plaything of sailors, until the trauma of it all left her with amnesia and she wandered through the streets of Tyre, disheveled and with a vacant stare. Her beauty and dignity that had been so much a part of her identity had been so stripped away that even close friends would scarcely have recognized her.

One former suitor named Menalaus, however, recognized her by a familiar turn of her head. He remembered in that one motion something about Helen of Troy, but Helen did not remember Menalaus. Over time he earned her trust by treating her with gentleness and respect. He constantly kept bringing up fragments from her former life, most of which did not register with her at first. Gradually, through his patient attention, Helen began to recognize a wisp from her past here, a shadow there, until finally she remembered who she was. Her disheveled and distant appearance soon turned into beauty and dignity again. And she began to be herself, the lovely Helen of Troy. When she remembered who she was, she knew what to do.

In the same way that Helen of Troy remembered her identity, even those of us with spiritual amnesia can remember our identity: beautiful reflections of God's image, people who belong to him. As the Psalms wash over us—disheveled and distant at times—they reconnect us to God through our experiences. Psalms don't take us out of the world or our situation but give us a new way of viewing God, our lives, and the world. The Psalms help remind us who we are: we belong to God. And when we know who we are, we know what to do.

Reflection

1.   Walter Brueggemann says grandmas and grandpas "are an active and intentional antidote for the amnesia that grandchildren too readily practice." How can the Psalms be an antidote to this kind of amnesia?

2.   How do Psalm 105 and Psalm 107 teach us about God?

3.   How do the Psalms shape our identity?

Action

1.   Read Psalm 105 and 107.

2.   What do the acts of God spoken about in these psalms reveal about him?

3.   Write how your story fits into the larger story of God's actions?

Chapter 12

LIVING WITH AMBIGUITY

*I never liked jazz music because jazz music doesn't re-
solve. But I was outside the Baghdad Theatre one night
when I saw a man playing the saxophone. I stood
there for fifteen minutes and he never opened his eyes.*

After that I liked jazz music.

*Sometimes you have to watch somebody love something before
you can love it yourself. It is as if they are showing you the way.*

*I used to not like God because God didn't resolve. But that was
before any of this happened.*[1]

—Donald Miller

E ven after the years of his hearing loss, Ludwig Beethoven wrote
some of his finest music. Though he was as deaf as a post, he would
stumble through the woods with complex scores echoing through his
head. In fact, some of his music written while deaf was too intricate
and expansive for the instruments in existence at the time. Beethoven's
music, in a sense, was a "prayer for better instruments."

Approaching God is something like a prayer for better instruments. We begin to glimpse something too large for our language, or even our understanding. These glimpses, however, expand our frame of reference, which then turns us into better instruments in God's hands.

On the journey of pursuing God through the Psalms, several important ideas have become like instruments that help us play new notes, listen for new melodies, and find both God's pleasure in us and deeper pleasure in our relationship with God.

The Psalms help us speak the unspeakable, explore the uncomfortable, freshen our prayers with new topics, open us to new purposes for prayer, get out of ourselves, give strength in our weakness, show where we belong—and the kicker is that people, including Jesus, for three thousand years have been finding that same depth in the Psalms. They have been praying for better instruments for three thousand years.

Living in the Psalms helps us in still more wonderful ways. The Psalms help us actually encounter the Holy One who frees us from the myth of certainty. *Praying the Psalms moves us toward the ability to live with ambiguity.* Some prefer to call ambiguity "transcendence" or "mystery" or "paradox." I like all three of these words, but I still like the word ambiguity best, because I believe with the prophet Isaiah that God's ways are not our ways, that he is beyond our ability to fathom, and we need language for that. Ambiguity works for me. I can almost hear God's voice saying, "Don't try to put me in a box of your own rational construction, whether it be Calvinist or Arminian or any other human invention." We cannot tame God, though humanity has tried for millennia to do so.

Some of the Psalms defy exegesis. They provide no answers. Rather, they leave us pondering. The clear meaning of some psalms eludes us. They speak in poetry or metaphor that is powerfully personal but inexplicable. Yet these psalms penetrate to levels of our soul deeper than logic, more poignant than reason.

Many modern believers have been reared under what theologians and philosophers call modernism. Modernism promises answers—precise scientific, factual answers that leave little to debate. Modernism assumes that if we approach things rationally, analytically, and logically that everything can eventually be explained to our satisfaction. We think that we need that.

God, however, will not cooperate! He will not subject himself to our formulations. He will not be confined or defined or defended. He is "too wonderful for me; too lofty for me to comprehend."

In his wonderful book, *Blue Like Jazz,* Donald Miller penned one short paragraph that hooked me immediately—the first lines of the book quoted at the beginning of this chapter. What got me is how he related jazz to God. He didn't like jazz because it didn't resolve. He didn't like God because God didn't resolve. Then in one moment, listening to a street musician, all that changed. No, he didn't learn all a sudden that God really did resolve. Instead, Miller experienced something real, listening to a man play the saxophone. He didn't just become more aware of jazz and how it doesn't resolve. His new awareness and appreciation showed him something entirely new about God.

Only an unresolved God is large enough to be worshipped. Only an unresolved God is mysterious enough to be truly beyond us. Only insight that is beyond analysis—so large it won't fit our categories and must be called ambiguous—is large enough to expand us and make us better instruments.

Even the mystery of our own hearts will not submit to such formulations. We human beings are too significant and too complex—too majestic, if you will—for our own comprehension. I guess I am a slow learner, but as I grow older, time is teaching me that many of my biggest questions will never be answered. Some of the largest truths about ourselves and about God are paradoxical, shrouded in mystery or unresolved ambiguity. But these truths expand us, take us deeper into the mystery of God, deeper into his heart.

Some of the Psalms take us deep into the mystery and the heart of God. One example is a contemporary lament song written by Randy Gill and based on Psalm 42. Randy Gill is a worship leader who knows the power of paradox and mystery. The last lines of this contemporary take on Psalm 42 echo with resolve to trust in a God who meets us even in the deep and mysterious places of our souls.

From the depths of my soul I cry out
From the depths of my soul I cry out
Lord, can you hear me?
    Have mercy, O God
From the depths of my soul I cry out

In the midst of the sea I cry out
    In the midst of the sea I cry out

Save me the water is over my head
    In the midst of the sea I cry out

There is a time to mourn
    There is a time to weep
There is a time for sorrow
    When deep calls to deep

In the moments of grief I cry out
    In the moments of grief I cry out
Have you forgotten me?
    Where are you, Lord?
In the moments of grief I cry out

From the depths of my soul I cry out
    From the depths of my soul I cry out
Still I will praise You, Lord
Still I will praise You, Lord

This contemporary psalm, "Deep Calls to Deep," helps us under-stand and live with the ambiguity, paradox, and mystery of God. Often psalms confuse and bewilder us, yet they draw us into encounter with a mysterious God who puts us squarely in the middle of conundrums such as these: First, how can a holy God also love us? Second, how can a God who knows everything we're going to do in advance also give us choices?

These psalms call us to admit with the prophet that "his thoughts are higher than our thoughts" and "his ways are past tracing out." They bring us before God who is utterly holy yet who loves us beyond comprehension. They leave us standing breathlessly before God who knows in advance everything we're going to do, yet bids us to make choices (Psalm 139).

God leaves us with no answer to this paradox, no effort to explain himself beyond this. He simply asserts that he is with us and this is who he is. In some ways, he leaves us betting our lives on God. I love the chorus from a song my son, Jon, has written that captures this courageous leap of faith:

And I'm not sure if there's a God in heaven
    And I don't know if there's a Lord above
And I can't prove that there's something worth living for
    But I'm betting my life on it, yeah
I'm betting my life on it[2]

Like God himself, the Psalms also sometimes raise huge questions for which they make no attempt to provide answers. They consistently affirm, however, God's wisdom and faithfulness and power and sovereignty and steadfast love. The psalmists repeatedly declare their resolve simply to trust in God. And they bid us do the same.

As I can personally testify after diagnosis of lung cancer and the failure of surgery to fully cure it—even when followed up with months of chemotherapy—there really is no one else to whom we can turn.

Why God allows things, why he chooses to heal one and not another, is a great ambiguity to me, one that the Psalms do not attempt to resolve. I have a friend who is also dealing with what his doctors call a terminal disease. He called recently to remind me of a great ambiguity in Ecclesiastes 7:14: "When times are good, be happy; but when times are bad, consider: God has made the one as well as the other. Therefore, a man cannot discover anything about his future." This verse states a huge ambiguity, a paradox—and offers no resolution—but simply nudges us to trust God.

God is all there is. There is nothing else to do but to bet our lives on him. Whether or not a cure lies ahead, only in him are we healed. Whether we live a while longer or die a while sooner, only in him are we healed.

Kip Long has bet his life on this ambiguous God who doesn't resolve. Kip is a worship leader and one of the most balanced and godly men I know. He participated in one of my mentoring groups. He did not know at the time how much he would need the Psalms to keep washing over him in the coming years. The road ahead for him was full of potholes and dangerous detours. During that mentoring year, Kip memorized Psalm 62. The certainty of God's fortress stood out to him in 62:5-7:

Find rest, O my soul, in God alone;
  my hope comes from him.
He alone is my rock and my salvation;
  he is my fortress, I will not be shaken.
My salvation and my honor depend on God;
  He is my mighty rock, my refuge.

But these were not the words that resonated with him when life took a tumble. He returned over and over to David's song for hope and assurance, but he related more and more to the words, "I feel like a broken down wall or a tottering fence." He felt as if his business was everyone's topic of conversation and so felt the same sinking suspicion that, "They are friendly to my face, but they curse me in their hearts."

"For several years," Kip said, "I have been waiting for the toxic fumes of mistrust, disappointment, and bitterness to evaporate from my marriage, but they haven't gone away. I have lost track of the times I asked God to breathe fresh air into our relationship, to heal my heart of painful wounds, to restore us. I'm in the middle of one of the most soul-numbing seasons of this life."

In this difficult season, Kip identified even more with Psalm 13, and borrowed David's words to ask God, "How long, O Lord? Will you forget me forever?" And truthfully, he felt as if God had looked the other way. Why was he waiting for divorce papers to be finalized? Why couldn't things be changed? His mind swam, his heart ached, and his soul was left reeling, but still he set Psalm 13 to music.

Kip says it's no coincidence that one year before his trials began, he spent several months in the mentoring group reading, praying, memorizing, and living the Psalms.

I have placed my life in God's hands, and I have no plan B. Without the Psalms, I would not know about the Good Shepherd who walks with me through the valley of the shadow of death. Without this prayer book, I would feel guilty about the "R-rated" prayers I have uttered toward God. But because I know the Psalms, I have peace in dark places. The script that I've been reading from has been ripped out of my hands. All I know is that God will give me the strength to be the best father, friend, ex-husband, son, and worship leader I can be. And because of the Psalms, I can say with confidence the words of Psalm 62:8, "O my people, trust in him at all times. Pour out your heart to him, for God is our refuge."[3]

What an amazing testimony! Kip tells about how God is both unresolved yet showing himself to be larger than life, bigger than our problems. The Psalms take us to the place where we can find comfort, even in the ambiguity of God. This leaves us more open to enter into the heart of God, because only he knows our future, and he is our refuge.

I'm particularly excited for you to go through the Action exercise at the end of this chapter. The exercise is supplied courtesy of my good friend, Reg Cox—who is not afraid of articulating the ambiguity and mystery of God, to cry out to him, to express the emotion of the psalmist.

Reflection

1. Describe a time when you expected God to resolve and it did not happen.

2. In what ways is it difficult to accept the way God leaves big questions unanswered?

Action

The following is adapted from a sermon by Reg Cox and used by permission.

1. Choose one of the forty-three personal lament Psalms: 3, 5, 6, 7, 9, 10, 13, 17, 22, 25, 26, 27, 28, 31, 35, 38, 39, 40, 42, 43, 51, 54, 55, 56, 57, 59, 61, 63, 64, 69, 70, 71, 77, 86, 88, 102, 109, 120, 130, 140, 141, 142, 143.

2. Read the psalm you choose.

3. Pray with the same emotion as the psalmist in your chosen psalm.

4. Write down some reflections in your journal. These reflections will be extremely valuable to you later. Perhaps you will one day share this time of trial with someone who will lead a church, make a decision not to commit a crime—you just don't know. But the emotions of life right now may be so hard that you'll forget this stuff, so write it down.

5. Sometimes it helps to try to summarize the sentiments expressed in a paragraph of one of the lament psalms in a few words. Something like, "The cry of one wounded beyond the

power to believe" or something else that might sound corny, but helps you track with the author.

6. Summarize all of your reflective thoughts and try to re-title the entire psalm. Somewhere in this exercise you'll be connected to the heart of God and some deeper places of trust and faith than you have ever possessed before.

7. Go outside and do something physical. If you sit around after this you might get depressed or become vulnerable to receiving messages God's not sending you. Exercise of any kind will help sort out your feelings. Pray: "Lord, I'm yours no matter what you do in this situation, but I need to be completely honest with you about how I feel about this situation. I think you have lost your mind this time. I can't see any possible way that the plan or direction you have for me right now makes a lick of sense." Let it fly. God can handle it.

Chapter 13

ENCOUNTERING THE HOLY ONE

They go from strength to strength
till each appears before God in Zion.
—Psalm 84:7

et's return finally to my most important discovery of all about the Psalms, and this is what this book is really all about. Even now as you may grow weary of hearing it, I feel I have not said it enough, could not say it enough.

The Psalms draw us into encounter with the Holy One. The goal is not the Psalms. The goal is God.

Certainly the Psalms reflect the delights and laments of God's people. And they alert us to a wide range of prayer concerns. The Psalms free us from self-centered prayers. They tune us in to the experiences of those around us. They link us up with the long story of the people of God. Psalms put us at peace with the ambiguity of God's designs.

Above all this, however, the Psalms sensitize us to the presence and nature of the Holy One and profoundly enrich our view of him. This deepens our trust in God, and paints new pictures of how to adore him. No matter how eloquent or how articulate our descriptions and definitions of God, they will never be nearly enough, nor totally accurate. The Transcendent One is larger than all of that. Even Scripture speaks of him only in metaphor.

God is a storm.

God is a door.

God is a warrior.

God is a rock.

God is a king.

God is a fortress.

God is a father.

Each of these metaphors—and each of many others—suggest only one glimpse of God, one limited point of observation. The psalmists know this. Their best words and metaphors only awaken our imaginations and longings in God's direction.

He is the God of both our highs and lows. God's presence and power have little if anything to do with whether or not we feel that he is at hand. Our moods may flap like a banner in the wind, but God remains constant—the solid rock upon which our house stands against hurricane force winds.

Throughout the book of Psalms, God is the center of focus. In each Psalm we find God receiving questions, doubts, praise, and lament. We find God is the center in many psalms, including the following:

The psalmist adores the Lord (Psalm 29).

The worshipers trust in God (Psalm 46).

The psalmist puts his hope in God even in the pit (Psalm 40).

David falls on God's Mercy (Psalm 51).

Faithful people receive the Lord's hand of blessing (Psalm 104).

The psalmist imagines God's infinite love and infinite forgiveness (Psalm 103).

Worshipers tremble at God's judgments (Psalm 76).

They are amazed at his majesty (Psalm 147).

And they are disappointed—even angry at God's sovereign choices (Psalm 42).

But the worshipers are renewed by steadfast love (Psalm 136).

On and on the brush moves across the ancient canvass, painting form, color, and tint to the divine portrait. The Psalms prompt us to notice God at work everywhere, in the everyday ordinariness of life and the glory of the ever-expanding universe.

Some people say we go to church to get all charged up to go out and face the real world. This is exactly backwards. God is the center of all reality. We go to church to be reminded of that fact. God is the center of our reality and our worship. This distinction matters enormously. Because if we lose confidence in his presence with us, we will begin to think that those things "out in the real world" really are real. When that happens, we are in deep trouble. God will remain, but we are in trouble if we forget where real life comes from.

We desperately need regular reminders of his presence and nature—else our attempts at worship drift downward from Yahweh wonder into golden calf country. Israel lost sight of the wonder of God, even at the foot of Mount Sinai where God was meeting with Moses.

They crafted an idol to look like a golden bovine. The focus shifted from God's transcendence to a tangible and convenient container for God. They were trying to worship God but not in the way he instructed them. The focus was more on themselves than on God.

Do we make idols in an attempt to worship God? As we wait upon God at the foot of the mountain, what shortcuts and tangible kingdoms do we buy into? Politics, education, security, jobs, children, homes? The Psalms continually remind us that worship is about God and not about us.

The Psalms so sensitize us to the presence and nature of God that they prompt us to notice him at work everywhere in the glories and the ordinariness of the ongoing and ever-expanding universe, the creation of God. God is God. He has always been God and keeps creating even now.

After Job had lost his family and property and had spent day after day trying to figure it all out with friends, the LORD answered him out of the storm (Job 38:2-7):

Who is this that darkens my counsel
with words without knowledge?
Brace yourself like a man;
I will question you,
and you shall answer me.
"Where were you when I laid the earth's foundation?
Tell me, if you understand.
Who marked off its dimensions? Surely you know!
Who stretched a measuring line across it?

On what were its footings set,
>   or who laid its cornerstone—
while the morning stars sang together
>   and all the angels shouted for joy?

God has always done his creative work to the backdrop of the praise of the heavens and earth. But we are not likely to have the ears to hear unless we live often in the mode of praise. The Psalms make us alive to God's presence, not merely in worship assemblies but in every sight and sound in nature around us.

For example, Psalm 29 gives us eyes and ears to pay attention to God everywhere. God's voice fills a summer storm. Psalm 29:3-9 says,

The voice of the LORD is over the waters;
>   the God of glory thunders,
>   the LORD thunders over the mighty waters.
The voice of the LORD is powerful;
>   the voice of the LORD is majestic.
The voice of the LORD breaks the cedars;
>   the LORD breaks in pieces the cedars of Lebanon.
He makes Lebanon skip like a calf,
>   Sirion like a young wild ox.
The voice of the LORD strikes
>   with flashes of lightning.
The voice of the LORD shakes the desert;
>   the LORD shakes the Desert of Kadesh.
The voice of the LORD twists the oaks

and strips the forests bare.

And in his Temple all cry, "Glory!"

We imagine the psalmist is somewhere in Lebanon on the lower slopes of Mount Hermon. He sees clouds gathering in the west, signaling a dark storm brewing over the waters of the Mediterranean Sea. The lightning flashes move eastward toward the mountains. As the storm reaches the slopes of Mount Hermon, the powerful voice of the Lord breaks the mighty cedars of Lebanon, makes Lebanon skip like a young wild ox.

Then the storm sweeps south toward the desert and the voice of the Lord shakes the desert of Kadesh. The storm finally crests in fury when the voice of the Lord twists the oaks and strips the forest bare of its leaves. Then as the storm reaches its final crescendo, all in his Temple cry, "Glory!" All of creation bursts into a Temple of praise.

Then the storm subsides and moves back out to the sea where the Lord sits enthroned above the flood and the Lord blesses his people with rest and peace. Through it all we see God's creative power and hear God's voice in the thunder and the wind. And God's power resounds in the splitting of the cedars and the quaking of the desert.

As the Psalms help us pay attention, we may see his life source in the emergence of every green leaf or fresh blade of grass, as my wife and I are learning to do through my illness. If we listen intently in the forest, we can almost hear the sound of leaves unfolding. The leaves are always in motion, unfolding, expanding. Motion takes life and energy. Where does this energy come from? From God himself. His very power is creating and energizing the quiet motion all around us.

In every green leaf and every unfolding, radiant blossom, in every bird in graceful flight, God is creating and energizing. When we enjoy a breathtaking sunset, we sense God's hand mixing the tint and hue to make it happen.

When alive to God's creative presence, we witness a miracle in every newborn baby. While we worship, God changes us. He creates things anew within us and around us. God's presence tunes our hearts to the heart of God so that our hearts thrill over what gives God pleasure. Our hearts are broken over what breaks God's heart. Our hearts feel pain over the things that cause God pain. So that as John Piper says, "The glory of God weans us from the breast of the world." The glory of God makes us people of compassion and justice. God speaks change into existence—God is the great heart-changer.

And he does all these things against a background of praise, as the morning stars sing together and all the angels shout for joy.

Reflection

1. How do the Psalms function in your life right now?

2. What changes are you ready to make to see the Psalms function differently for you, your family, church, or small group?

3. How do you deal with a God who does not resolve all the big questions of life?

Action

1. Write a phrase from each of the psalms listed below.

2. With each phrase, pray a prayer on behalf of others, expressing the great benefits of God's love, mercy, blessing, and hope if we trust in him.

3. Some of the phrases express doubt and fear of God's judgments. Include the spectrum of emotions from these psalms in one continuous prayer.

Adoring God—Psalm 29

Trusting in God—Psalm 46

Hoping in God—Psalm 40

Accepting God's mercy—Psalm 51

Receiving God's hand of blessing—Psalm 104

Standing in awe of God's holiness—Psalm 103

Trembling at God's judgments—Psalm 76

Feeling disappointment, even anger at God's sovereign choices—Psalm 42

Being renewed by God's steadfast love—Psalm 136

AFTERWORD

As I grow older, my mind often goes back to the images in the Psalms. The image of Psalm 84 is of pilgrims on a journey to the dwelling place of God. And on the journey to where they think God lives, they find God along the way in creation, in the midst of suffering, and in reflective pools of autumn rain. The psalmist shouts, "How awesome is your dwelling place, O LORD Almighty!"

As with the psalmist, so I yearn for that dwelling place—my heart and my flesh cry out to the living God. Some of you might confuse the dwelling place of God with heaven, but that's just it—the dwelling place of God is not heaven, neither is it earth. God created those places for us to dwell with him, but he is not contained in them, nor will he be contained. The dwelling place we're in pursuit of is not Jerusalem, not simply some place in our hearts, not a pool in the Valley of Baca. The dwelling place we seek is God himself. The psalmist is looking for a dwelling, a shelter, a strong tower, a mighty fortress—in God himself. Psalm 84:5 speaks of that longing for God's dwelling place:

> Blessed are those who dwell in your house;
>> they are ever praising you.
> Blessed are those whose strength is in you,
>> who have set their hearts on pilgrimage.

On this pilgrimage to God, the great surprise is that he has been with us all the way. We're all on a journey to the cities of God, but don't confuse this with heaven. Our dwelling is not a place. Our dwelling is God himself, as Psalm 90 says,

> Lord, you have been our dwelling place
> > throughout all generations.
> Before the mountains were born
> > or you brought forth the earth and the world,
> > from everlasting to everlasting you are God.

Looking back over my shoulder to the winding path we've taken through the Psalms, I realize even more now that I haven't given you a systematic study of the Psalms. I did not set out to do that. I did not dissect every psalm, nor did I go through them in order. Instead, I set out on this journey to show you an adventure of a lifetime. The adventure is not tied up in reading, praying, singing, and memorizing—those are just tools of the road toward living the Psalms and ministering with them to others. The real adventure is finding the heart of God—the rush of the trek is that God is bigger than any mountain we could climb, higher than any rocket we could design and propel into space. God fills the space of the earth and bursts out of the temples we have made. His universe can't expand quickly enough to hold him.

The Psalms give us a pathway to pursue God. Come and join the throng of worshippers past, present, and future who are pursuing God himself as their dwelling place. This is a trip you just can't miss.

PSALMS FROM THE ROAD

The following are ministry field reports about how my brothers and sisters are living in and ministering out of the Psalms. These friends have graciously recounted their journey of pursuing God by using Psalms to read, sing, pray, memorize, and minister to others.

Psalm from the Road by Lee Patmore

Psalms has born more spiritual fruit in my life than I ever imagined. In my quest for a deeper spirituality, I had ventured into psalm territory only on rare occasions. When I dipped my toes into the Psalms, I didn't feel at home. The imprecatory psalms were offensive to me; I didn't know what to do with them in light of the teachings of Christ. Plus, the poetic language wasn't the language of my heart. "Just give it to me straight," was more my style. I was a New Testament Christian—the less than subtle implication was that the Old Testament was second-rate content. The Psalms had three strikes against them.

I became a Christian at nineteen years of age. Although I've had my share of ups and downs in the three decades of following Jesus, I can honestly say that I never went through a conscious time of rebellion against God. But I have battled long against my own legalism. Something, however, was missing. I yearned for a deeper, richer prayer life. I studied Scripture and gained amazing insights from God, but relationship with the Father was lop-sided. He did most of the talking. I thought about God frequently; I prayed to him throughout the day.

Still, I felt a deep void in my prayer life. I never got lost in pouring my heart out to God.

The pivotal moment for me in deliberately choosing to spend time in the Psalms was when it was pointed out to me that Jesus had immersed himself in the Psalms. He had read them, memorized them, and prayed them. I realized that Jesus' words of agony on the cross were not some carefully rehearsed quotes that the divine Son said merely to fulfill a couple of ancient prophecies. They were the psalmists' words of prayer that the Son of God had embraced and made his own. He, like thousands before him, grew up memorizing and meditating on the Psalms.

I had never been a fan of memorized prayers. By their very nature they seemed second rate at best, vain repetition at worst. This new insight exploded that myth. If Jesus prayed a memorized prayer on the cross, as he was pouring his heart out to the Father during his greatest hour of need, how could they be in any sense second rate?

Armed with this new insight, I began to journey through the Psalms. When I found one that seemed to connect with me, I would spend time daily praying it, first for me and then for others. In addition I would begin to memorize the psalm, one verse per day until I had the whole psalm locked into my soul. I was careful always to do my memorization work out loud, speaking the words with as much passion as I could muster.

I repeated this exercise week after week for one year. During that time, I experienced several firsts. I had never shouted a prayer before. Now, shouting a prayer is a regular occurrence. The Psalms demand shouting once they get into your soul. I had never openly expressed doubt or fear in prayer before. It's hard to find a psalm that doesn't take you on that journey. I often laugh out loud as I recite a psalm. Most often this is a laugh of bold confidence; Psalm 27:1 often does this to me. Praying the Psalms has given me the words to pour out my soul to God, whatever the present circumstances. Daily I journey from doubt to faith as I recite psalms; I move from fear to confidence and weakness to strength. Psalms that once meant nothing to me—I cannot imagine living without them.

Since I answered the call to ministry a few years ago, it's often been lonely, sometimes terrifying. I'm frequently challenged to the core of my soul. I don't know where I'd be without the Psalms to allow me to express my heart to God—and teach me how. Like all spiritual disciplines, this one doesn't come naturally. On the first read, a psalm often comes up flat to me. Fifteen minutes of memory work later, the same psalm never fails to unveil my heart—another wonderful gem of a psalm. I choose to spend time in the Psalms every day. I still frequently approach prayer half-heartedly but the Psalms never leave me there.

I don't fully understand Paul's words concerning the Spirit's intercession in our prayers, but if one text could describe what praying the Psalms has meant to me, it's Romans 8:26: "In the same way, the Spirit helps us in our weakness. We do not know what we ought to pray for, but the Spirit himself intercedes for us with groans that words cannot express."

Today I began a new psalm. "To you O Lord, I lift up my soul . . . ." Once again the Psalms have given new life to my prayers. On a two-hour car ride to pick up my parents at the airport, I spent the whole time reliving the psalms I have memorized. Early Sunday morning, I was on my knees in the sanctuary, hands outstretched in the dark as the Psalms helped me to express my yearnings for my Father. No one will ever take the Psalms away from me!

Lee Patmore is a minister in a church that straddles Alberta and Saskatchewan.

Psalm from the Road by Jackie Halstead

My journey with the Psalms is similar to that of others—as I have experienced the suffering of life, I have "discovered" the Psalms. Before this discovery, I thought of it as the long book in the center of the Old Testament that was a challenge to get through in my annual Bible reading. It had pretty language, but I did not connect with it in a personal way. The discovery came through the painful experience of the stillbirth of our second baby.

As a young minister's wife, my life was devoted to God. I had been faithful to the best of my ability and relished the opportunity to work alongside my husband for the kingdom. At some level, I realize now that I thought I had a special status and would be exempt from suffering. God was rewarding me for my devotion with a carefree life and would continue to do so all my days. The death of our baby put this devotion in a tailspin. How could God repay me in this way? What did I do to deserve it? I did not believe that God caused the death, but I knew that God is God and he could have prevented this tragedy. In my grief and anger, I decided that God did not deserve my faithfulness. I distanced myself from him, all the while keeping up appearances in our work with the church.

I finally came to my senses three years later due to the extreme loneliness I was experiencing. I had never lived without God, and the three years alone had been excruciating. I realized that the only thing worse than enduring pain was enduring that pain without God. That was when I "discovered" the Psalms. In my grappling with how to come back to God, I encountered the book of Psalms. How amazing it was to see my thoughts—fear, anger, pain—written on those pages. Had they always been there? How bold David was in his wrestling with God. Did I dare confront God in the same manner and yet praise him in the next breath? Was this portrayal a possibility for me of a different, fuller relationship with God?

This discovery began the lifelong process of redefining my relationship with God. I learned in this instance that God is at the center of this relationship, not me. I learned that when I experience joy, I cling to God, and even more importantly, when I suffer, I cling to God. Life is not about devoting myself to a God who will meet my needs; it is about offering myself as an instrument to be used for God's glory and his kingdom.

In this release, I found freedom. My discovery of the Psalms and the relationship I saw in those passages allowed me to let go of my small plans and seek to be useful as a conduit of God's love and grace. It was no longer about me, but about God.

My perspective regarding this large book in the middle of the Bible changed dramatically. It is now a constant companion on my journey and remains close to my heart. Twenty years after the stillbirth of our daughter, life has given me sufficient opportunity to test the relationship I learned from the Psalms. The key is keeping God at the center, as Psalm 63:1 articulates so well:

O God, you are my God,
    earnestly I seek you;
    my soul thirsts for you,

my body longs for you,

in a dry and weary land

where there is no water.

Jackie Halstead is Chair of the Marriage and Family Department at Abilene Christian University, Abilene, Texas.

Psalm from the Road by Albert Lemmons

Prayer, faith, and fasting have been on my heart forty years. I've lived and breathed and studied these topics, and have been honored to conduct hundreds of ten-hour seminars on prayer. In these seminars, without exception, the eighth hour, my final hour on Saturday evening, is spent praying the Psalms. I pray the following psalms: 43, 32, 51, 34, 73, 15, 20, 90, 91, 16 and 22, closing with 23, the Shepherd Psalm. Following that, prayer sessions often continue for another hour or so and occasionally until midnight. I never know what shape a miracle will take. A friend calls it a rainbow of grace.

As the heart panteth after the waterbrook,

O God, my soul longs for you.

My soul thirsts for you as in a dry and weary land.

Why are so many downcast? So disturbed?

Yes, I know that many to whom I minister are suffering as tears fall like the rain, but you O God, help my audience understand how to place faith and hope in you, mender of lives. I see David, the writer of so many psalms of conflict, tranquil in his closing years in an unbroken walk with God. Only grace made that possible for him and for me. There is peace and undiminished trust in God.

Abba Isaac said, "The man who prays the Psalms will make the thoughts of the Psalms his own. He will sing them no longer as verses composed by a prophet, but as born of his own prayers. At least he should use them as intended for his own mouth and know . . . that they are being fulfilled in his daily life."

So, may you grow in peace and trust in God as you make the words of the Psalms your own prayers.

Albert Lemmons is a prayer conference leader in Nashville, Tennessee.

Psalm from the Road by Chris Goldman

Growing up, preachers at my home congregation didn't preach much from the Old Testament and only referenced the Psalms, usually at a funeral or a wedding. I can't remember ever hearing a lesson coming from the Psalms as the textual base except for Psalm 23. My experiences really didn't offer much to draw from, with the exception of a couple of college classes that led me into the Psalms in a new way. However, as part of a mentoring group I was meeting with, Lynn challenged us to memorize a different psalm every month. The power of a psalm rises exponentially when committed to memory. Psalms are poetic. This means they speak to the heart in a powerful way—especially when placed permanently as a memorized prayer. When we know a psalm intimately enough to pray it from the heart, the psalm takes on a life we cannot imagine.

For eight months, before preaching a message at the Pepperdine University lectures, that's where I placed Psalm 103: in my heart. After preaching the message on Psalm 103, one of my teachers who had taught me in a course on the Psalms commented on the "depth" of the message that captured the "heart" of Psalm 103. I'll never forget that comment. Capturing the heart of poetry isn't my strength. By placing Psalm 103 in my heart, however, I connected with the heart of the psalm.

Those of us who aren't naturally oriented towards the "heart and soul" but primarily lean towards "mind and strength" need the Psalms so we can hear and feel the heart of God. Without them, our faith leans toward mental pursuits, losing the pursuit of and the mystery of God. The Psalms bring us back to the beauty and mystery.

Chris Goldman is a minister in Seattle, Washington.

Psalm from the Road by John Pickens

Whether praying the Psalms or memorizing them, the result is the same: defibrillation of my frenetic soul.

Whether I am seeking wisdom or the reclamation of my spiritual identity, my mind is refreshed and my spirit is renewed. The Psalms are God's rain upon my arid wasteland of pain, self-disappointment, and fear.

If I had to choose one psalm that has inspired me consistently over the past eight years, it would be Psalm 84. I memorized this psalm in 2003 while a part of one of Lynn's mentoring groups. It never grows old, never ceases to inspire me in my ministry and personal life, and never leaves me tethered to the demon that often oppresses me.

The soothing, reassuring cadence of Psalm 84 points me heavenward with its repetitive reference to God's dwelling place, where even the sparrows long to live and raise their young. One day in the residence of Jehovah is better than one thousand days in luxurious accommodations elsewhere. God is both ruler and protector and he blesses the man that trusts in him.

Oh, I can listen to the beat of that drum every day!

John Pickens is a minister in Oklahoma City, Oklahoma.

Psalm from the Road by John French

On a farm in West Tennessee in the middle of the woods there stands a special tree. The tree is not impressive by any measure; in fact it is deformed. A larger tree fell across this tree when it was a sapling, bending it over. This created a curvature at the base of the trunk.

What makes this tree special is that my father, now in his eighties, came across this tree one day on a walk through the woods. The curvature made a perfect seat for him to take a rest. While sitting there he took a moment to pray. Over time the tree became a favorite place for my father to pray. One day when riding horses on the trail, my father showed me the curved tree rest—a place of prayer. Now it has become a place of prayer for me, too.

Over the past few years I have invited many friends, family, and folks I want to know better to ride horses on our farm. At the end of our ride, just before heading to the barn, we stop by what we have named the "praying tree." We stopped by this tree so often that my old mare stops all on her own. She knows a prayer must be said before she can return to the barn. At the praying tree, I have often shared my favorite psalm. Psalm 139 is my favorite because it reminds me of God's constant love, care, and presence in my life. I am always blessed by praying this psalm at the praying tree, and those riding with me those days are blessed as well.

There is something about memorizing a psalm that makes it become a part of us. The psalm seems to become part of our DNA. It has a way of seeping from our pores at precisely the right moment, when no other words seem appropriate. Memorizing the psalms gives us the perfect words to minister, bless, encourage, and comfort others during times of need. There is something special about connecting with the words of the Psalms that have blessed God's people for generations. Even our Lord cried out a psalm while nailed to the cross.

I encourage everyone to take some time to memorize a psalm. Perhaps you can share your favorite psalm with someone at a "praying tree" in your neck of the woods.

John French is a firefighter/paramedic and landscaper in Memphis, Tennessee.

Psalm from the Road by Jim Martin

It was raining hard that evening, and I could barely see the middle line on the two-lane Tennessee highway. I was on my way to the hospital in Columbia, Tennessee. I had just received word that a twenty-six-year-old woman from our church was near death. She was dying of cancer and our little church had been grieving with her.

I was a young minister, preaching for a little storefront church about thirty minutes from Columbia. I had never been called to the hospital like this before. In fact, I had never seen anyone die. I had never preached a funeral.

The woman died about an hour after I arrived at the hospital. Many family members and friends were present in the waiting room, supporting those closest to her. A few minutes after her death, the friends began to quietly leave, giving the family some privacy.

I wondered what I was supposed to do. A very wise and gentle nurse approached me and said, "You probably want to take the family into the chapel for a few minutes." The nurse quietly asked the family to follow her to the nearby chapel. I stood at the door of the little chapel as they filled in, one by one. The room was completely quiet.

I saw a large Bible at the front of the chapel. I opened it to Psalm 23 and read the ancient words of that psalm. I then prayed for the family.

That rainy night, in the midst of this family's grief and my own fear, I found that the Psalms gave me words where I had none. In fact, I saw Psalm 23 provide a word from God to a family who desperately needed to hear his voice.

A light came on for me that night. I learned that the Psalms are the words of God that can speak to the tender places of the heart. This lesson spoke powerfully not only to the value of the Psalms in my ministry, but in my life as well.

Years later, I would learn just how valuable the Psalms could be for nurturing my heart on quiet mornings. I had been in one of Lynn Anderson's mentoring groups where he had challenged each of us to read the Psalms.

Early one morning, with a cup of coffee in one hand and a yellow highlighter in the other, I began reading the Psalms. I began with Psalm 1 and underlined every word in the psalm that either named God or was an action or description of his character. I did this each morning, working through five psalms each day. After reading these Psalms and marking these words, I skimmed through the texts that I had read. I allowed these words and phrases to shape my prayer for the morning.

Finally, after reading the entire book of Psalms, I began flipping through the pages of the book. The book was saturated in yellow where I had highlighted word after word. I was overwhelmed by how the Psalms were saturated with God! I have since done this exercise on a number of occasions using different translations.

The Psalms have encouraged me to pay attention to God. He certainly is paying attention to me. His words in these Psalms continue to provide me with strength, direction, and encouragement.

Jim Martin is a minister in Waco, Texas.

Psalm from the Road by Kip Long

I write this in the middle of one of the most soul-numbing seasons of my life. For the past four years I have been waiting for the toxic fumes of mistrust, disappointment, and bitterness to evaporate from my marriage, but they haven't gone away. I have lost track of the times I asked God to breathe fresh air into our relationship, to heal my heart of painful wounds, to restore us. More than once I opened my Bible to Psalm 13, and borrowed David's words, "How long, O Lord?" Will you forget me forever?" And truthfully, I feel as if he has looked the other way. What happened here? Why am I waiting for divorce papers to be finalized? Why couldn't things be changed? My mind is swimming, my heart is aching, and my soul is reeling.

I don't think it is coincidence that one year before my trials began, I spent several months in a mentoring group with Lynn Anderson reading, praying, memorizing and living the Psalms. Little did I know that God was preparing my heart for a hurricane!

One of the psalms I memorized was Psalm 62. Time and time again I have returned to David's song for hope and assurance. I can relate when he says, "I feel like a broken-down wall or a tottering fence (v. 3)." I have felt like my business has been everyone's topic of conversation and so I have felt the same sinking suspicion that, "They are friendly to my face, but they curse me in their hearts (v. 4)." But God sends his peace to my soul through the words of verses 5-7:

I wait quietly before God, for my hope is in him.

He alone is my rock and my salvation, my fortress where I will not be shaken.

My salvation and my honor come from God alone.

He is my refuge, a rock where no enemy can reach me.

When I allow God to be the source of my salvation, I have no need to seek it elsewhere. I have placed my life in his hands, and I have no plan B. And when God is the source of my honor, I don't have to worry about my approval rating. I can be on the "who's who" list or the "who's he?" list and not be tossed back and forth by the ebb and flow of public opinion.

Without the Psalms, I would not know about the Good Shepherd who walks with me through the valley of the shadow of death. Without this prayer book, I would feel guilty about the "R-rated" prayers I have uttered toward God. Without this timeless hymnal, I would not know that God likes songs that go back and forth from a minor key into a beautiful major chord. But because I know the Psalms, I have peace in dark places. Because I've read David's prayers, I feel justified to say what I need to say to God. And because I sing from the same hymnal as all my faith heroes, I can sing my songs with confidence, knowing that he appreciates every note.

I don't know what my life holds. The script that I've been reading from has been ripped out of my hands. All I know is that God will give me the strength to be the best father, friend, ex-husband, son and worship leader I can be. And because of the Psalms, I can say with confidence, "O my people, trust in him at all times. Pour out your heart to him, for God is our refuge."

Kip Long is a worship leader in Memphis, Tennessee.

Psalm from the Road by Marvin Bryant

My own most recent, profound experience with the Psalms took place during a five month forced absence from preaching due to surgery on my vocal cords. There were some good times while I was out, but there were also a lot of difficult times. The examinations, surgery, and recovery hurt physically. The ordeal hurt emotionally. What I love to do and feel called to do was taken away from me. I felt weak, unproductive, useless, vulnerable, whiny, uncertain about my future as a preacher, and uncertain about my calling. My sinful self-reliance was exposed. My tendency to try to gain validation through what I accomplish was exposed. I had been praying that God would open my heart and help me to feel the feelings I had stuffed for years and get over the perfectionism I used to cover up my feelings. This ordeal certainly addressed all that.

While I couldn't preach, I could read. I read lots of good books and I read THE Good Book a lot, especially the Psalms. I used the Psalms to form many of my prayers to God. One psalm that I especially related to was 40. Like the author (David?), I was in a slimy pit (40:2). I cried out to God and waited for him, sometimes patiently (40:1), sometimes not. After months of prayer and gradual recovery, I was allowed to preach again. Even though I couldn't say he gave me a firm place to stand, because I wasn't out of the woods yet, I could say God lifted me out of the slimy pit.

But the most wonderful part about it is the way God worked through my ordeal to pierce my ears (40:6) and write his word on my heart (40:8). In ancient times, when God answered prayers, it was customary to offer him sacrifices and thank offerings, but the Psalmist realized that that's not the effect God wanted to have on him. Instead, God wanted to open his ears and write the word on his heart, that is, give him the desire to do God's will. I found the same thing to be true. I found myself growing much hungrier for God and for God's word. I found myself hearing it more with my heart and not just my intellect. In my college days I was caught up in academia, not realizing it was a way of hiding from my feelings. In the last few years I have realized the need for the word to be written on my heart, and I have been praying that God would write it there. During my wilderness time I realized God was doing to me what he did to this Psalmist—using adversity to write the word on my heart.

The psalmist said God put a new song in his mouth (40:3), which was probably literal. For me it is metaphoric—instead of a song, God gave me a message through this ordeal. I learned that while we are suffering, God is composing—he's giving us a song or message or story in our hearts. Like the psalmist, I have the privilege and responsibility of speaking in the great assembly (40:9-10), and I gained a powerful message to share. The more aware I am of my weakness, the more powerful God makes the message. The same thing is true in personal conversations as well. When opportunity arises to talk about God working on us or about weakness or about faith, I now talk about them in a much different way, sometimes with tears in my eyes, which is pretty amazing in my case. Isn't this close to what C. S. Lewis said? God whispers to us in our pleasures, speaks in our conscience, but shouts in our pain. It is his megaphone to rouse a deaf world (or church!).

The second half of Psalm 40 reminds me that the journey isn't over. More struggle likely lies ahead. And sadly, but not surprisingly, even after having the word written on his heart (40:8), this psalmist still sinned (40:12) and found himself in another mess. So he once again did what he had done before—cried out to the Lord (40:13-17).

That season of challenge for my voice and my soul taught me two particular truths from Psalm 40. These two truths were written on my heart clearly:

First, we really need to trust God.

Second, God works through weakness.

Marvin Bryant is a minister in San Antonio, Texas.

Psalm from the Road by Philip Claycomb

For years I had a begrudging and reluctant relationship with the Psalms. I frankly didn't care much for them. I could read them and not feel a thing. As far as I was concerned they were about as interesting and helpful as the sterile landscapes I still encounter when I wander through certain tracks of Leviticus and Numbers. Yes, an occasional surprise might crop up here and there. But by and large, I just saw words upon words piled up one against another. For whatever reason they didn't speak to me. I continued to read them because I felt I ought to, but I didn't expect to discover much in them.

This changed when I decided to let Rueben Job and Norman Shawchuck (*A Guide to Prayer for Ministers and Other Servants*) serve as my quiet time guides for the following year. The format of their guide required that I read the chosen psalm each day for an entire week. I remember chafing at this turn of events, but I stuck with my commitment. Imagine my surprise when I discovered that the psalm that had been wooden and voiceless on Monday was opening up and speaking to me by Thursday. As the year progressed I found myself returning to those psalms that had befriended me only weeks before. By the end of that year several of these psalms had become my steady companions. They gave me the words to express what I was feeling before God.

At the end of that year I determined to get better acquainted with all of the psalms. I set out on what I figured would be a three-year study of all 150 psalms. I decided to spend one week with each psalm, reading it daily, then studying it with the help of a handful of commentaries I selected. I usually studied the psalms by reading first those commentaries that deal with the more dense and technical matters. Then I turned to the less complicated and more devotional commentaries.

My goal was to emerge at the end with a handle on all 150 psalms. I wanted to give each of them an individualized title that would summarize the theme as well as express what it says to me.

All in all, my intentions worked out, but not as neatly as I had imagined. Instead of three years (roughly one psalm per week) I ended up taking just over seven years. The pace of one psalm per week soon relaxed into a quiet and leisurely stroll through the Psalms. I stayed with each song for as long as I felt gripped by its melody. Once I felt I had explored the individual terrain each psalm offered, and had identified a working title for it, I would move on. But as the process played out I found myself becoming less driven, more reflective, and better able to witness what God was doing in my own life and that of others around me.

It has been several years since I completed my study through the psalms. But I would say that I am still journeying through them and letting them guide my prayer. I continue to pray my way through them on a daily basis. I will occasionally recommit myself to reading them through in one month (reading and praying through five psalms each day). At other times I return only to the particular psalm that best expresses my situation or feelings at that time.

My friend Lynn Anderson got me started memorizing them several years ago, and in this way I find myself praying them both privately as well as when I'm praying for others. I spend a great deal of time traveling and find that the relative isolation of an airliner makes an excellent "cell" in which to meditate on or memorize a psalm. I find myself pointing the leaders I coach and mentor to these psalms. I hope to help them discover that these prayers can speak *to* us as well as *for* us.

I find myself regularly retracing old territory in the psalms. I find myself rediscovering old treasures I had forgotten, or new ones I have overlooked. And all the while I continually find myself prompted to rename them yet again. The titles I gave them years ago seem entirely insufficient to express what I now find when I linger within them. Again and again the psalms reveal new or subtly different messages that I had been incapable of hearing years before. I suppose that's why I keep coming back—they just keep revealing more and more.

Given a chance to start all over again in a long walk through the Psalms, I certainly would! There is, however, one thing I would do differently if I had a chance: next time I'd record the titles in my Bible in pencil and not ink!

Philip Claycomb is the director of Nexus: Church Planting Leadership in Dallas.

Psalm from the Road by Grady D. King

The cool, soft rain dances lightly on the tin roof just before light of day in Zambia. I am here with friends sharing faith and hope in Jesus Christ. It is a short-lived time, but I know God is present in the dancing rain. I drift back to sleep and awake to the dawn of a new day—birds sing, a rooster crows, but mostly there is stillness.

It is a morning for the Psalms—for listening to ancient friends of faith once again. The Psalms give a voice to my soul. When I cannot pray, they speak for me. When my words fall limp in a season of crippling fear, they call me to deeper trust. When I seek words to express exuberant joy or deep sorrow, they echo in my soul as friends who stick closer than a brother. When sin grabs me around the neck choking the life of God out of me, they are present. Along the trail of faith and disillusionment, my ancient friends of faith comfort, challenge, and cleanse my spirit.

At some point in my faith journey, Psalms ceased to be merely ancient poetry and became friends to my soul. These friends keep inviting me to places in my own soul that I do not want to go but cannot resist—places of pain, disillusionment, and confession. These friends rekindle fire in my bones when the embers of ministry are dying. I cannot imagine what it would be like to try to minister without the Psalms, much less to seek God and follow Christ.

Several years ago I realized that I had been doing full-time ministry for twenty-five years with nothing more than a short vacation or seminar each year. I was tired, about to begin a doctor of ministry program and, admittedly, running on empty. I confessed it to my shepherds, as if they didn't already know and asked for a one month sabbatical. They were gracious and encouraging. Off to Colorado I went. A beautiful cabin, mountains, and time to rest, read, think, and write. I decided to eat healthy, walk daily, fast some, and spend time in the Psalms. My method: read, pray, and sing the Psalms—out loud, beginning with Psalm 1. Whatever melody came to me or seemed to fit, I would sing. Sometimes it was simply more like a chanting stream of words than a discernible melody. I began with Psalm 1 and read until my ancient friends spoke to my soul.

Sometimes I would read several psalms before praying or singing. It was a hard discipline. My mind wandered all over the place. I even pondered if this was a waste of time. I could not slow my mind down from all the ministry stuff back home. And then there were those strange, even carnal thoughts flooding my soul as I read ancient words and songs of faith. Where were these coming from? What was going on? Frustration increased. My spirit was so tightly wound that it took God three days to unwind me through the Psalms and rest in him. Finally, he did. There was plenty of talking back to God—of pouring out my soul.

One morning I took a long drive to the Black Canyon of the Gunnison. It was early April, blue skies, but high winds. Wind warnings were posted for the canyon rim. I came upon an overlook named "pulpit rock"—an appropriate place to stop for a minister. Getting out of the car, I stood overlooking the grandeur of the Black Canyon. It was God's pulpit and oh how he proclaimed his sovereignty to me. I felt small. The strong, cold wind died down. With the warm sun on my face, my soul erupted in song: "How Great Thou Art." Tears flowed. And echoes of the psalmists poured from my lips. Joy restored. Soul alive. Fire re-kindled. That was nine years ago and the Psalms as ancient words from ancient friends still speak. And when they do, they are not so ancient. I cannot imagine life without them.

The Psalms have been conversation partners in many a hospital room, phone calls, notes of encouragement, and mentoring groups with church leaders. They punctuate funerals and even weddings. And their stories of faith, doubt, fear, and joy are shared in countless sermons with struggling believers and broken churches. What the Psalms say about God shapes not only what I believe, but how I go about ministry. Jesus read, quoted, and lived the Psalms. I can do no less.

A few months ago I buried a good friend. His name was Jack, a school superintendent in the same district for forty-four years. Colon cancer took him in less than a year from the time of diagnosis. He was not particularly a church-going person, but a man of high moral character, integrity, and grit. He was very private and did not trust most ministers or politicians. We became friends anyway. One day his wife called and said, "Could you go see Jack in the hospital." The permission to visit list was small—only four or five people. We talked openly and

TALKING BACK TO GOD

frankly about his prognosis, regrets, and relationship with God. He said, "You know how I have struggled with prayer and church, but I do believe in God." And then his large hand grabbed hold of my forearm and said with voice trembling, "Pray for me," immediately followed by, "Just be with me in the end." I knew I was on sacred ground with Jack. I prayed. And when the words came, they were those of ancient friends—the Psalms. Ironically, he requested several psalms be read at his funeral. I did. With the community and school district filling the church, the words of Psalm 46 and Psalm 23 reverberated in the souls of grieving people. Even me.

Since it is by God's mercy I minister, I do not lose heart—to a large extent because I can talk back to God pouring out my soul. I thank God for these ancient friends with their ancient words. Let everything that has breath praise the Lord.

Grady D. King a minister in Irving, Texas.

Psalm from the Road by David Gregersen

In times of trouble the Psalms have always provided me just the right words I need to pour out my heart to Our Father. I learned this early in my ministry as our four-month-old son Jay died of a rare disease on August 23, 1980.

My words dried up, but my emotions were at flood stage. The Psalms rose to the surface. The psalmist's ancient thoughts and emotions became mine, channeling my sorrow and confusion upward to God. Psalm 13 was one I memorized and prayed. Perhaps King David expressed those very words when his infant son died.

Fast forward twenty-eight years to August 24, 2008. That was the last day I would be with my eighty-two-year-old father, Jacob Gregersen. Just two weeks before, on the day of their sixtieth wedding anniversary, my parents heard the doctor's diagnosis. Dad had acute leukemia. He would have six weeks to six months to live.

I was home on an extended furlough from Zambia and it was time to return. September 1 was the day Linda and I were to fly back after an unexpected five months away.

That final day together Dad and I talked of faith, God's love, heaven, and the love between father and son. I asked to hear him pray one more time. We decided that since no one knew exactly how fast the leukemia would move through his body, we would say goodbye now, knowing that this would be our last time together on this side of eternity. We comforted each other with the thought that this would be "our last goodbye." Living apart as we had for so many years, we had said goodbye to each other many times. But that day in August would be our last. We also found comfort in the knowledge that the next time we would see each other would be the welcome home in the presence of our Lord, never having to say goodbye again.

We wanted to stay spiritually connected to each other while we waited for his departure. The Psalms provided that connection even though we were ten thousand miles apart: he was in Searcy, Arkansas, and I was at Namwianga Mission in Kalomo, Zambia. We decided that until he died we would read a psalm each day starting with Psalm 1. Our spirits would be connected through the ancient words of the psalms.

Dad whispered the words of Psalm 1 along with me as I read them out loud to him. And then we said goodbye.

Five weeks later I got the call telling me that he had died. It was early morning in Africa, and I had not yet read the psalm for the day. I opened my Bible to Psalm 26. This was the last psalm he had heard. Two lines from the ancient psalm spoke truth to my grieving soul:

I have trusted in the LORD
> without wavering.

I love the house where you live, O LORD,
> the place where your glory dwells.

I was flooded with comfort from the Lord as I read the final words of Psalm 26, words that describe Dad's eternal life experience.

My feet stand on level ground;
> in the great assembly I will praise the Lord.

And that is where we will say our next "Hello."

David Gregersen is a missionary in Zambia.

Psalm from the Road by Reg Cox

The lament psalms are worship in the midst of suffering. The book of Psalms is a combination of emotionally charged worship, prayer, and gut journal. It is a collection of Hebrew worship songs that were used for singing or chant worship.

Prayers in the Psalms include the heart cries from men and women of faith expressing their desires before God during joy, trial, and times of planning for the future. The lament psalms touch on all these but especially give us insight into the hidden struggles of men and women of faith. They open us up for such foreign dimensions of prayer as cursing, weeping, emotionally charged outbursts, rants filled with rage and fantasies of violence, and the listing of grievances against God. If Job had used psalms to aid him during his faith journey it would have been lament psalms.

The lament psalms can be described as "praying at the edge." The prayer or psalm is often filled with challenges, bartering, and something we'd have to consider an outright threat. There just isn't anything in Scripture as raw as the lament.

Out of the 150 psalms, conservative estimates place the number of laments at fifty-seven or thirty-eight percent of the Psalms. Scholars divide the lament psalms into "personal" and "communal" laments.

When David is feeling overwhelmed and all alone as his son searches to kill him, the father and king writes Psalm 3. Here we get insight into his heart and thoughts. David feels surrounded, but then his faith is strengthened when he remembers the fact that God is stronger and will defeat his enemies—both physical and spiritual.

How a father regains faith when it is his own son hunting him down, I don't know. But David lets us journey with him as he seeks a path through a situation where victory will only lead to a future of grieving over his lost son. Sort of the original catch-22.

But that's real life—the lament psalms don't leave us with a bunch of spiritual happy talk, quotable faith pick-me-up sayings, or even answers. Laments just point us to the only possible resource for dealing with this kind of pain. And we are left with only two options:

Option 1: Give up, give in, and forget life.

Option 2: Get up, get on with it, and follow God until he shows us the way.

The lament psalms slap us in the face, kick us in the backside with a size 14 boot. Laments invite us into the fury of spiritual transformation—not to lie upon the lilies awaiting a cup of warm milk. Communal laments give the community words to speak when grieving. In Psalm 137 the community weeps and cries out in captivity. They request vengeance against their captors and their faith is stirred, remembering that God alone is the one in control of everything—even when Jerusalem lies in ruins and they are bewildered by his seeming inaction. This is troubling—so troubling that the whole community cries out to God together in lament.

Lament psalms are not for the spiritually faint of heart. If your prayers are dominated by what you want God to do for you instead of what you want God to do through you at any cost, you might want to just skip laments for your devotional reading. This isn't the kind of Scripture you go to for a good night's sleep.

This is the kind of stuff you plug into because you want the very structure of your faith reformatted by a blast of Holy Spirit voltage so shocking and overwhelming that you either vaporize upon contact or become purely fanatical. This kind of reading will jolt you awake and melt your affection for a shallow and empty addiction to the world.

Want to go to the next level and get serious about your faith in God? Well, the journey to that kind of existence leads one to travel through the land of the "dark night of the soul," in the words of a poem by St. John of the Cross. In that territory the only vocabulary that makes sense is lament.

These are not pretty lines of poetry. Don't go looking for flowery language extolling the "beauty" or "loveliness" of God here. This is more the motorcycle gang language section of the Bible. The angels in heaven must have pleaded, "Do we have to let David write this stuff?"

Blunt, brutal, honest, gut wrenching, take-the-gloves-off, get real—these are the sentiments of lament. There is little emotional room left in the hearts of the suffering to sit around and wonder if this thing you're feeling is politically correct or if it's going to hurt someone's feelings or not. The whole world around you has just been crushed and you just don't care how what you're about to say is going to impact those in listening range. They just better get out of the way or become prepared for the spray because a volcano of raw emotion is about to blow. And unless you blow you cannot proceed to the place of desperation. And if you never venture to the place of desperation you can never rip off the scab of indifference, the scar of apathy, or the slavery nose ring of compromise.

Lament is the prayer of one who cries out in one breath, "Isn't there any other way we can do this, God?" and in the next sentence sincerely pleads, in the words of Christ, "but not my will but yours be done." Lament strips away the false from the true in us so completely that we are ready to be honed into a seriously undefeatable weapon in the arsenal of God's world-changing leadership team.

The lament prepares us for a lifetime of attentive spiritual compliance to the will of God with a passion and desire for obedience that goes way beyond duty. We are now compelled to obey because we have glimpsed the possibilities of God from the bottom of the pit of despair. That perspective is unmatched for unleashing the plans of God in your life.

The goal of the lament psalm is not information—it's transformation. Go to these psalms and ask God to forge in you a new soul, a new faith, and a new desperation to believe and follow him to the cross.

207

Personal Laments: **Psalms 3, 5, 6, 7, 9, 10, 13, 17, 22, 25, 26, 27, 28, 31, 35, 38, 39, 40, 42, 43, 51, 54, 55, 56, 57, 59, 61, 63, 64, 69, 70, 71, 77, 86, 88, 102, 109, 120, 130, 140, 141, 142, 143**

Penitential psalms (repentance): **Psalms 6, (32), 38, 51, 102, 143**

Cursing psalms: **Psalms 12, 35, 58, 59, 69, 70, 83, 109, 137, 140**

Protestations of innocence: **Psalms 17:3-5, (18:20-24), 26:1-6, (41:12), 44:17-22, 59:3c-4a**

Reg Cox is a minister in Denver, Colorado.

Psalm from the Road by Greg Taylor

For two decades I've run between two poles of belief about the Psalms.

Either . . . the Psalms are ancient, distant, and irrelevant to faith.

Or . . . the Psalms are timeless, touch our humanity, and are full of God's life.

For many years I thought no good theological stuff could come out of the Psalms, so why read them? Sure, psalms made good songs, and lots of worship songs were based in the Psalms. While I enjoyed singing those songs, really reading them only confused me. I wondered why Bible publishers pasted the Psalms onto the back of perfectly good New Testaments. I knew Psalm 23. That was about it.

After all . . . okay, I'll just say it: psalms are poetry. How could I love psalms if I hated poetry?

That's when I had sort of a Donald Miller *Blue Like Jazz* moment of my own. Not about jazz but about poetry. I read a poem that overturned a thousand English classes where I was forced to write haiku or diagram rhyming couplets. I never thought I'd pick up a book of poems, but one day I did. A book called *A Liturgy for Stones* (Telford, Pa.: DreamSeeker Books, an imprint of Cascadia Publishing House, 2003) by David Wright and read, "My Friend at Firestone Asks about Poems." The voice in the poem is that of a factory worker asking a poet if there's any room in his poems for stuff that's real to him. The poem slapped me in the face and showed me once and for all—though I had been told many times in school and didn't listen—that poems are stories about real life . . . and they don't have to rhyme, but neither does life seem to rhyme either.

Wright's poem helped me realize that the Psalms are also poem songs about real life. David is caught in crimes and cries out to God for mercy in Psalm 51. One son is dead and later another son wants David dead—more psalms come out of these grievous paradoxes in David's life. Real life and real psalms. I could read this stuff.

So for two decades now I've read five psalms a day off and on, and tried to memorize them; but I'm either a better forgetter than these other guys in this book who memorize psalms, or I haven't worked hard enough at memorizing. I can sure tell that Lynn's life is saturated with the Psalms because he is a person of peace who has discovered the second truth: that Psalms are timeless, touch our humanity, and are full of God's life.

Maybe I should have memorized Psalm 42 a long time ago. Then I would have known all those years that the song, "As a Deer Pants for the Water," which is based on Psalm 42, is only shorthand and doesn't scratch the surface of the psalm. Discovering real life in Psalms has been a find of a life-time. The depth of emotion and angst the Sons of Korah must have felt when they wrote this psalm! Were these guys the factory workers asking if God had any place for them? Wasn't it they who said, "My tears have been my food day and night, while men say to me all day long, 'Where is your God?'"

Psalm 42 is a particularly memorable psalm for me in ministry because of two entry points in my life and church. My friend Randy Gill unearthed this psalm for me when he wrote the lament song, "Deep Calls to Deep." He wrote the song— quoted earlier in this book—before the events of 9-11, but in those dark days to come, the song became a lament over the crisis in our world.

Years later Psalm 42 voiced a deep sorrow for my church community that had been left speechless by the suicide of a teenager. Reading the words at the funeral ministered healing without avoiding the real pain penetrating all of us, particularly the family.

Now I've left the far pole—that way of thinking that the Psalms are only ancient poetry better left on papyrus. The psalms have run like a bead of glue uniting ancient people of faith with faithful people today—from the factory worker to survivors of 9-11 or suicide or war.

I'm finding that Psalms speak to people in hospitals, at funerals, in crises—in all the times when we least expect to hear them. And that's when they strike us and bring tears to our eyes like someone slapped us across the face.

Greg Taylor is a minister in Tulsa, Oklahoma.

TAKING THE PSALMS
TO HEART

Objective: Develop a life of praying and memorizing the Psalms, and then mentor and equip others to do the same.

First Month

Step One: Reading the Psalms

Pray at least one Psalm each day. Pray the Psalm three times. Start at the beginning of the book of Psalms, and take one each day in sequence, 1-150.

First Reading: Read the psalm aloud, slowly and thoughtfully, to get the sense of it. While you read, sense the sheer adoration in the psalms—even if expressed in ways that you don't understand. Relax and surrender to God's will and open your heart and mind.

Second Reading: Pray the psalm aloud slowly, reflectively—in the first person. Make the prayer your own now. Don't hurry through the prayer. Wallow in it. Savor it. Mean it.

Third Reading: Pray the psalm aloud slowly, reflectively—in the second person. Now take the prayer to a new place, praying the psalm as an intercessory prayer on behalf of someone else.

Key: Let this psalm springboard you into the rest of today's prayer. Pray about the current issues and persons in your life that the psalm has brought to your heart. The words in the psalm have already suggested at least one theme. Notice how events of the day lead you back to one of the themes. Come back to that place of prayer on that theme.

Step Two: Memorizing the Psalms

1. Pray your daily Psalm.
2. Memorize all or part of a Psalm each month. You can do it! The key is daily repetition.
3. Read new material aloud five times then quote it aloud five times on the first day. The following chart shows one method for reading and quoting, decreasing daily repetitions throughout the month.
4. Add new material each day until you memorize the whole psalm or section.
5. Notice in the chart below that you will be decreasing your readings and increasing your quoting.
6. Add at least one verse of new material each day until the whole psalm is fixed in your memory.
7. Once the psalm is fixed in your memory, only quote it once by memory each day.

	Read Aloud	Quote Aloud
1st day	5x	5x
2nd day	4x	5x
3rd day	3x	4x
4th day	2x	3x

5th day	2x	3x
6th day	1x	2x
7th-30th day	1x	1x

Tips for Memorizing the Psalms

1. Choose your favorite Psalms. Choose short ones or sections of long ones—sections of at least five verses. No certain order is necessary unless you feel more ordered by making your own sequence.

2. Break material into small parts of six to fourteen words, meaning one or two lines.

3. Do not exceed thirty minutes a day memorizing—at least in the first few weeks.

4. Read aloud correctly with the proper expression—with eyes on the words.

5. Then look away to quote aloud and with expression from memory.

6. If you make an error while quoting, immediately correct the error four times—aloud.

7. Each day, add a few small parts—as time allows, or attention span lasts.

8. Any new small parts added from day to day are to be read and quoted, repeated exactly, as the material used on the first day.

After Thirty Days

Once material is fixed in memory, set aside time each month to review previously memorized psalms. For most people who pursue this exercise for a year, the Psalms they have covered will never be forgotten.

You will find your mind running through a psalm in the night, while you drive down the street, as you go about your daily tasks, when you relax. If you get behind, don't give up. Celebrate what God does through this discipline.

Third Month

Step 3: Pass it on

1. Train at least two more people to pray the psalms in the manner you have learned.
2. Even before you begin training, "pray up" a list of people with whom you might share this skill. I call this a GGTW list: Guys and Gals to watch. Begin today.
3. Ask God to bring to mind people, or lead you to people for your list—people you think might have some natural affinity with you, or might be interested in learning this classical prayer life. Write the names down.
4. As your list of names forms—even before you approach them— start praying for the persons on your list.
5. Ask God to help you discern the right time and the right way to approach them.

Fourth Month

Step 4: Duplicate Yourself

1. Set a time to explain to others the value of praying the Psalms. For example, use the table of contents of this book for help in explaining the benefits and values of pursuing God through the Psalms. After explaining, ask if they want to accept at least a three-month challenge with you.

2. Assign them at least a part of what has been assigned to you above, and set a time to meet with them again—ideally once a week, but at least every two weeks, but not less than once a month. This regular accountability and sharing will help all of you gain insights from the Psalms and memorize them together.

Fifth Month

Step 5: Multiply Yourself

1. Challenge each person to train at least two more people to read, pray, sing, and memorize the Psalms.

2. Offer to be their coach in the early stage of their process, for as long as they may wish or is practical and expedient.

3. Encourage them to keep passing it on. Remember 2 Timothy 2:2, "And the things you have heard me say in the presence of many witnesses entrust to reliable men who will also be qualified to teach others."

[Adapted from *You Can Memorize God's Word* by Marlin Hoffman]

ENDNOTES

PART I: HUNGER

Chapter 1

1 Eugene Peterson, *Answering God: The Psalms as Tools for Prayer* (New York: HarperCollins, 1989), 36-37.

2 Walter Brueggemann, *Praying the Psalms: Engaging Scripture and the Life of the Spirit,* 2nd ed. (Eugene, OR: Cascade Books, 2007), 7.

Chapter 2

1 Dallas Willard, *The Spirit of the Disciplines: Understanding How God Changes Lives* (New York: HarperCollins, 1988), 152.

Chapter 3

1 Thomas Wolfe, *You Can't Go Home Again* (New York: Harper & Brothers, 1941), 706.

2 Michael W. Smith, "Ancient Words" from the *Worship Again* CD, Reunion Label, 2002.

3 David Wray, Notes on Spiritual Formation, Mentoring Partners' Retreat, 2008.

4 Wray, 2008.

PART II: VOICES

Chapter 4

1 Email from Bobby Deagan to Lynn Anderson.

Chapter 5

1 Simon Chan, "The Dark Night of the Soul," in *The Contemporaries Meet the Classics on Prayer,* compiled by Leonard Allen (West Monroe, LA: Howard Publishing, 2003), 194.

PART III: HELPS

Chapter 7

1   Eugene Peterson, *Answering God: The Psalms as Tools for Prayer* (New York: HarperCollins, 1989), 89.

Chapter 8

1   Walter Brueggemann, *Praying the Psalms: Engaging Scripture and the Life of the Spirit*, 2nd Ed. (Eugene, OR: Cascade Books, 2007), 17.

2   Author unknown.

3   John Killinger, unpublished sermon manuscript on Psalm 23.

4   Lynn Anderson, speaking at 1999 Pepperdine University Bible Lectures on "The Lord Is My Shepherd."

5   Victor Frankl, *Man's Search for Meaning* (New York: Washington Square Press, 1984), 62-63.

6   Leroy Garrett, speaking at Abilene Christian University Summit, September 2008.

PART IV: MINISTRY

Chapter 9

1   Dietrich Bonhoeffer, *Life Together* (Harper & Row, 1954), 44-50.

2   Scot McKnight, *Praying with the Church* (Brewster, MA: Paraclete Press, 2006), 53-54.

3   McKnight, 54.

Chapter 10

1   C. S. Lewis, *Christian Reflections* (1967).

2   Peter Greer and Phil Smith, *The Poor Will Be Glad* (Grand Rapids: Zondervan, 2009).

PART IV: WONDER

Chapter 11

1   Lynn Anderson, *Longing for a Homeland* (West Monroe, LA: Howard Publishing, 2004), 137-139.

2   David Fleer and David Bland, ed., *Reclaiming the Imagination: The Exodus as Paradigmatic Narrative for Preaching* "Antidote to Amnesia," Walter Brueggemann (Danvers, MA: Chalice Press, 2009): 7.

3   *Reclaiming the Imagination: The Exodus as Paradigmatic Narrative for Preaching* "Antidote to Amnesia," Walter Brueggemann.

4   David Fleer and David Bland, ed., *Reclaiming the Imagination: The Exodus as Paradigmatic Narrative for Preaching* "Basket of Memories," Lynn Anderson (Danvers, MA: Chalice Press, 2009), 172-174.

5   Eugene Peterson, *Answering God: The Psalms as Tools for Prayer* (New York: HarperCollins, 1989), 91.

Chapter 12

1   Donald Miller, *Blue Like Jazz: Nonreligious Thoughts on Christian Spirituality* (Nashville: Thomas Nelson, 2003), 2.

2   Unpublished song, copyright Jon Anderson.

3   From an email from Kip Long to Lynn Anderson, 2010.

Additional Resources

Brueggemann, Walter. *The Message of the Psalms.* Augsburg Old Testament Studies. Fortress Press, 1985.

Crenshaw, James L. *The Psalms: An Introduction.* Grand Rapids: Eerdmans, 2001.

Mays, James Luther. *Psalms,* Interpretation, a Bible Commentary for Teaching and Preaching. John Knox Press, 1994.

Peterson, Eugene H. *Answering God: The Psalms as Tools for Prayer.* HarperOne, 1991.

Schaefer, Konrad. *Psalms,* Berit Olam Series. Liturgical Press, 2001.

ACKNOWLEDGEMENTS

We began this book with Michelangelo's sense of closure. Let me end by returning to Michelangelo. He was the sole author of his statement about King David. But it would not be entirely honest for me to claim to be the sole author of this David-related book. In fact, this book is a collaboration with many people. So let me name and thank some of the collaborators—at least the first three rows of them.

Thank you to Dr. John T. Willis—my friend, shepherd, and Old Testament scholar—and to Dr. Tony Ash, who first opened my heart to the power of the Psalms.

Later, Randy Harris, theology professor and popular speaker, alerted me to the riches of reading the Psalms aloud. He pointed out that by reading five psalms a day, we move through all one hundred fifty in a month.

Thanks also to Eugene Peterson for his book *Answering God*, which provided me a roadmap to pray and sing the psalms. For Peterson, most of the Bible is God's word to *us*, but the Psalms are *our answers back to God*. This insight from Peterson is what inspired the title of my book, *Talking Back to God*.

The preparation for two assignments in the late 1990s launched my journey of praying and memorizing the Psalms, which continues to this day. The first assignment was four keynote messages on worship for a July 1999 Nashville conference called *Jubilee*. My preparation took me through numerous volumes on worship, sharpening my focus and further whetting my appetite for the adventure of praying and singing the Psalms.

And my thanks to Dr. Jerry Rushford, director of the annual Pepperdine Bible Lectures, who gave me the second assignment: he asked me to speak on Psalm 23 for what he called, "The Last Pepperdine Lecture of the Millennium."

For the guidance of these dear Pilgrims of the Psalms, I shall forever be grateful.

Thanks also to the people who carefully read my manuscript; you have offered invaluable insights: Mark Abshier, Carolyn Anderson, Jon Anderson, Marvin Bryant, Charles Coil, and Reg Cox.

And thank you to the persons who offered endorsements. You have given my feeble offering enormous credibility.

Thank you to the persons who sent in your Psalms from the Road. Your chapter may be the best one of all.

An even bigger thanks to Greg Taylor. When I was unable to finish the manuscript by deadline, you stepped in as a writing assistant and first editor. You took such great pains to "preserve my voice" that I doubt the reader can tell which sections are yours.

Thank you to Leonard Allen of Leafwood Publishers, who believed in this book from the get-go and who continually "kept all the wagons headed west."

Finally, thank you to my beloved Carolyn. You have been my soul partner for these fifty-three years. You have been my best friend, my cheerleader, and the most significant collaborator for everything I've done.

And blessed be the name of our glorious Lord.

Lynn Anderson

Dr. Lynn Anderson is the founder of Hope Network Ministries, with a mission for coaching, mentoring, and equipping Christian leaders. His fifty years in the ministry include church planting as well as serving as senior minister in churches both in the U.S. and in his native Canada. In addition to personally coaching church leaders all over the world, Lynn has taught graduate ministry courses as an adjunct professor at Abilene Christian University and Pepperdine University.

He has authored several well-known books including *If I Really Believe, Why Do I Have These Doubts?*, *The Jesus Touch*, *The Shepherd's Song*, *They Smell Like Sheep*, and a follow-up *They Smell Like Sheep Volume 2*, subtitled *Leading with the Heart of a Shepherd*. His most recent book is titled *Exit Stage Right: Conversations on Finishing Strong and Dying Well*, co-authored with Darrel Gilbertson. He also contributes to *Wineskins Magazine* and several other periodicals and web sites, as well as an ongoing blog on his own website, www.mentornetwork.org.

Lynn has consulted with hundreds of churches, coaching leaders through transition and equipping them with shepherding skills and other tools for spiritual formation. Lynn and his wife Carolyn live in San Antonio, Texas.

CPSIA information can be obtained
at www.ICGtesting.com
Printed in the USA
FFOW02n0954220816
26986FF